THE WORLD CHAMPIONSHIP BOXING QUIZBOOK

THE WORLD CHAMPIONSHIP BOXING QUIZBOOK

introduction by

JOSÉ TORRES

and foreword by

JACK DEMPSEY

by Bruce Nash and Julian Compton

Drake Publishers, Inc. / New York · London

ACKNOWLEDGMENTS   A special thank-you is extended to Mr. Nat Loubet, President and Editor of The Ring Magazine, for providing the photos which appear in this book.

Published in 1976 by
Drake Publishers Inc.
801 Second Avenue
New York, N.Y. 10017

All rights reserved.
© Copyright in 1976 by Bruce M. Nash

Library of Congress Cataloging in Publication Data

Nash, Bruce M
    The world championship boxing quizbook.

    1. Boxing--History--Miscellanea.   I. Compton, Julian E., joint author.   II. Title.
GV1121.N27   796.8'3'09   76-16369
ISBN 0-8473-1311-5

Printed in the United States of America

To Greg, my "little" brother, who finally learned how to whip me

And Ann, who wishes boxing was never invented

CONTENTS

Foreword by Jack Dempsey — xi

Introduction by Jose Torres — xiii

The Preliminaries — 1

		Questions	Answers
1.	Sending the Crowd Home Early	3	92
2.	Third Man in the Ring	3	92
3.	Fight Sites	4	92
4.	The Great White Hopes	5	93
5.	Counting For the Knockdowns	5	93
6.	The Friday-Night Fights	6	94
7.	Below The Belt	6	94
8.	...Eight, Nine, Ten -- Yer Out!	7	94
9.	Brother Warriors	7	95
10.	Million Dollar Gates	8	95
11.	Ring Aliases	8	95
12.	The Great John L.	9	95
13.	Gentleman Jim	9	96
14.	Ruby Robert	10	96
15.	The Boilermaker	10	96
16.	Tiny Tommy	11	97
17.	Li'l Arthur	12	97
18.	The Manassa Mauler	13	97
19.	The Fighting Marine	14	98
20.	The Boston Gob	14	98
21.	The Livermore Larruper	15	98
22.	The Brown Bomber	15	99
23.	The Brockton Blockbuster	16	99
24.	The Rabbit	17	99
25.	The Ugly Bear	18	100
26.	Smokin' Joe	18	100
27.	Pugilistic Potpourri	20	101
28.	In This Corner...: Photo Quiz I	21	102
29.	Bare Knucklers	31	102
30.	Rules of the Game	31	102
31.	The Doughboys Return	32	103
32.	Going the Distance	32	103

VIII / Contents

		Questions	Answers
33.	We Wuz Robbed!	33	103
34.	Tale of the Tape	33	104
35.	Boxing Peculiarities	34	104
36.	The Near-Champs	34	104
37.	Tinsel Town Boxers	35	104
38.	Nicknames I	36	105
39.	Nicknames II	36	105
40.	Fight Lingo	36	105
41.	The Michigan Assassin	37	106
42.	Mama's Boy	37	106
43.	Sugar Ray	38	106
44.	The Old Mongoose	38	107
45.	The Boston Tar Baby	39	107
46.	Hammerin' Hank	39	108
47.	The Toy Bulldog	40	108
48.	The Unknown Triple-Champ	40	108
49.	Fistic Firsts	41	109
50.	Return of the Champion	41	109
51.	Will the Real World Champions Please Stand Up?	41	109
52.	Olympic Champions	42	110
53.	Pick the Decade	43	110
54.	Home Town Boys I	43	110
55.	Home Town Boys II	44	111
56.	Main Events: Photo Quiz II	45	111
57.	Ring Deaths	70	112
58.	Boxer vs. Slugger	70	112
59.	Spot the Division	70	112
60.	The Heavyweights	71	113
61.	The Light-Heavies	72	113
62.	The Middleweights	72	114
63.	The Welterweights	72	114
64.	The Lightweights	72	114
65.	The Featherweights	73	115
66.	The Bantamweights	73	115
67.	The Flyweights	73	115
68.	The Junior Weight Titles	74	116
69.	The All-Time Greats	74	116
70.	Battles of the Century	75	117
71.	The Cornermen I	75	117
72.	The Cornermen II	75	117

		Questions	Answers
73.	Big-Time Operators	76	118
74.	Outside Notables	76	118
75.	The Barons of Boxing	77	118
76.	Unsung Giant-Killers	77	118
77.	Bowing Out	78	119
78.	The Final Count	78	119
79.	Their Post-Glory Years I	78	119
80.	Their Post-Glory Years II	79	120
81.	Trademarks	79	120
82.	You're the Judge	80	120
83.	Dirty Fighters	80	120
84.	Remember When...?	81	121
85.	Win, Lose, ...Or Draw	81	121
86.	Fix!	82	121
87.	Memorable Quotes	83	122
88.	Pugilistic Styles	83	122
89.	Pick the Round	83	123
90.	Classic Fight Series	84	123
91.	Championship Reigns	84	123
92.	International Flavor I	85	124
93.	International Flavor II	85	124
94.	Boxing Tidbits I	86	124
95.	Boxing Tidbits II	86	125
96.	Boxing Tidbits III	87	125
97.	Pick Your Own Top Ten	87	126
98.	Muhammad Ali Super-Quiz I	88	126
99.	Muhammad Ali Super-Quiz II	88	127
100.	Muhammad Ali Super-Quiz III	89	127

The Verdict   129

FOREWORD

Having been associated with boxing for as long as I can remember, I naturally take an avid interest in anything that is written about or on boxing. The World Champion Boxing Quizbook has been long overdue and I feel it will appeal to all sportsminded people who can read and want to know ...

It is obvious that Mr. Nash and Mr. Compton have exhaustively and thoroughly done their homework, proving through their efforts that all that is connected with boxing is indeed timeless. I am sure the World Champion Boxing Quizbook will be a winner by a K. O. as it will be the perfect refresher if one doesn't peek at the answers ...

Jack Dempsey

INTRODUCTION

You are reading this book because you probably like the boxing game. You could be a very ardent boxing fan. You could be one of the many who once loved the sport of flat noses.

But whatever your category, you probably agree that boxing is a rough, tough business. In fact, you may say that the most outstanding ingredients in a boxing contest are: blood and sweat, lumps and pain, the separation of the senses.

In short, you probably are a member of an overwhelming majority of boxing people who see boxing as a brute sport.

But that does not mean that there are not areas of the sport you like. Who would dare to say that Sugar Ray Robinson was not a beautiful thing to watch? Or what about the punching power of Joe Louis; the five-punch combinations of Floyd Patterson; the perseverance of Rocky Marciano; the finesse, class and graceful arrogance of Muhammad Ali?

All the special qualities in these fighters and many others you do appreciate and remember. You also remember the fighters who lost with dignity and the ones who scored impressive victories.

That memory and that experience makes you a boxing fan. And if you are part of the many who would not miss a fight on the television set, or who attend local fights at the arena, well, then, that makes you an "expert".

If you fall into this category then you are expected to have boxing arguments at home, at your favorite bar, your office or the factory.

You are no different from, say, the typical sportswriter, the typical boxing manager, trainer or promoter. You can talk as equals with boxing commissioners or executives, for they know as much about boxing as you do. In fact, their sources of knowledge are the same as yours.

Basically, you and all boxing people see us pugilists, as super machines with enviable physical superiority. Only a very few see us as human beings with brains and feelings.

Our physical mechanism is praised. But what about our intellect? What about the qualities which really make us tick?

Boxing's enemies as well as the game's advocates, not excluding the "experts", all derive their boxing knowledge from what they see.

Unfortunately, my dear reader, what you and the rest see is no more than thirty percent of what's happening in the ring. And if you decide to take a close look at the remaining seventy percent of the fighter's struggle, you still might not see it. But, you may.

Do you know, for example, that the first thing a fighter faces when he decides to make boxing his livelihood is fear? That the total dedication of a fighter who wants to be a champ comprises hidden qualities like determination, desire, guts and especially will.

Do you know that the basic difference between an ordinary fighter and a champion is the latter's ability to *control* these hidden qualities? And what about the unconscious development of the sense of anticipation? Which is to *know* what your opponent is going to do *before* he does it.

When we are in the ring we must be able, ready and willing to follow instinct with great faith. We must change pattern, predict with utmost accuracy coming events under devastating psychological pressures.

Only then can a boxer reach a level of competition in which the physical mechanism becomes practically irrelevant.

Now the fighter makes it or simply becomes an eternal opponent. For now it is no longer a contest of physical abilities, but a contest of will. Who really wants to win?

All of a sudden the jab and the hook, the uppercut and the bolo-punch, the straight right and the combination punches become the secondary asset to victory.

This stage of no-return includes one's ability to resist being knocked out, the refusal to become tired: perseverance is indispensible every second of the contest. One must continue at it until one's opponent succumbs one hundred per cent or succumbs *one* per cent. For that is the difference between victory and defeat.

In short, the final stage for one whose goal is the championship, is one of character. For one is now into the profound and complex level of the boxing plateau -- the contest of character between two young, healthy, conditioned men in search of ultimate victory.

You may see it as a physical victory. But we champions see it, consciously or subconsciously, as a victory of character and the control of abstract motivations in every champion's head.

José Torres

THE PRELIMINARIES

It is the most electrifying moment in all of sport. A hush falls over the crowded arena as the house lights yield to a single spotlight shining down on the ring announcer. His greasy, slicked-back hair glistens under the bright overhead lights. The fighters dance with their backs to each other in their respective corners. The steady clatter of ringside typewriters keys the mounting tension to a fever pitch. The referee stands alone in a neutral corner of the ring, stealing nervous glances at the unfamiliar faces in the crowd. Finally, the dull clang of the ringside gong cues the ring announcer to grab the overhang microphone. His shrill voice crackles through the smoke-filled arena as hearts pound mercilessly in the throats of the wild-eyed spectators: "L-a-adies and gentlemen...Fifteen rounds of boxing...For the heavyweight championship of the world!!"

From bareknuckle fights in the mud to a multi-million dollar ring war staged in darkest Africa before a worldwide closed-circuit television audience, championship boxing has captured the imagination of the American public. No other sport can match the "sweet science" for the concentrated excitement which is crammed into the brief span of a fifteen-round championship bout. There are no halftimes, rest periods, teammates to rely upon, time-outs, substitutions, or best-of-seven series to redeem yourself if you fail to survive the initial test. In boxing, man is pitted against man in an intense psychological and physical struggle for superiority within the lonely confines of a roped-in canvas battleground. The slightest edge in either combatant's speed of hand and foot, stamina, courage, punching power, or ability to withstand punishment often spells the difference between ring ignominy and championship status.

Boxing has enjoyed a rich and glorious history...John L. Sullivan's braggadocio...Jack Johnson's stormy reign as boxing's first black champion...spindle-legged Bob Fitzsimmons' sneaky solar plexus punch...Jack Dempsey's savage two-fisted attack...flamboyant Tex Rickard's multi-million-dollar promotions...deadpan Joe Louis' bone-crunching power...Rocky Marciano's swarming body assault...Smokin' Joe Frazier's relentless bore-in style...and Muhammad Ali's machine-gun jabs and ballet-like grace.

THE WORLD CHAMPIONSHIP BOXING QUIZBOOK is your ducat for a ringside seat to look back in on the classic fights and legendary champions of yesteryear. You'll crowd into arenas all over the world as you test your ring savvy out on elusive questions such as these:

- Who was the only man to defeat Rocky Marciano in the prize ring?
- Who won the heavyweight championship of the world while seated on the canvas?
- What fight attracted boxing's first million dollar gate?
- What fight produced a record number of 49 knockdowns?
- Who was the first man to knock Muhammad Ali off his feet in a professional fight?

Toll up your points scored on each of the 100 challenging quizzes to obtain the officials' verdict at the end of the book. Are you up to the challenge? Stay on your toes and be prepared to take your best shots at this flurry of nostalgic brain-teasers from Boxing Past.

1. SENDING THE CROWD HOME EARLY (10 pts.)

How many of these explosive one-round knockouts can you recall?

1. His knockout of challenger Jem Roche in 88 seconds of the first round stands as the fastest recorded finish to a heavyweight championship fight.
2. Jimmy McClarnin kayoed this namesake of an early heavyweight king to win the welterweight title on May 29, 1933 in Los Angeles, California.
3. "The Old Master" captured the world lightweight crown on a one-punch knockout in the first round of his "fight" with Frank Erne on May 12, 1902.
4. Light-heavyweight champion Georges Carpentier successfully defended his title against this 152-pound "smashing, bashing, crashing, dashing kid" by scoring a first-round knockout when the challenger turned to the referee to protest a call.
5. As a last minute substitute for his brother Joe, this middleweight champion was kayoed in the first round by southpaw upstart Al McCoy on a jolting left uppercut to the windpipe.
6. George Foreman knocked out this "King" in his first heavyweight title defense on September 1, 1973 in Tokyo, Japan.
7. Four months after winning the lightweight championship on a one-round knockout of Sammy Mandell on July 17, 1930, he lost the title to Tony Canzoneri on a first-round kayo.
8. Known as "The Brooklyn Terror," he won the bantamweight title by knocking out Pedlar Palmer in one round on September 12, 1899 in Tuckahoe, New York. When he couldn't make the weight as bantam champ, he abandoned his title and proceeded to defeat George Dixon in eight rounds for the world featherweight crown on January 9, 1900.
9. Which one of the following boxers did *not* suffer a first-round knockout in a heavyweight title fight? (a) Sonny Liston (b) Max Baer (c) Max Schmeling (d) Jersey Joe Walcott (e) Bill Squires.
10. Ever since Corbett kayoed Sullivan on September 7, 1892 in twenty-one rounds, there have been only twelve heavyweight title fights to end by knockout in the first round. Which of the following heavyweight champs is responsible for producing five of these early kayos? (a) James J. Jeffries (b) Tommy Burns (c) Jack Dempsey (d) Joe Louis (e) Rocky Marciano (f) Muhammad Ali.

2. THIRD MAN IN THE RING (15 pts.)

Identify these unsung referees who changed the course of boxing history with their split-second ring decisions.

1. What celebrated fight promoter refereed the "Great White Hope" match between black champion Jack Johnson and former titleholder James J. Jeffries?
2. Who refereed most of Joe Louis' big fights?
3. What referee sued Ali because of the champ's critical remarks of his handling of the Wepner bout?
4. Who refereed the first Ali-Frazier "Battle of the Century?"
5. While refereeing the Joey Maxim-Sugar Ray Robinson light-heavyweight title fight, he collapsed from heat exhaustion and was replaced after the tenth round. Four rounds later, Sugar Ray himself was overcome by the scorching temperature

and was forced to end his quest for a third world title. Who was the ref that was stricken with heat prostration on this bizarre night of boxing?
6. Who refereed the controversial "Battle of the Long Count" at Soldier's Field, Chicago on September 22, 1927?
7. Following a protest by Arturo Godoy's manager Al Weill, referee Arthur Donavon was barred from the second meeting between the Chilean powerhouse and heavyweight champion Joe Louis. Who replaced Donavon as third man in the ring for this bout?
8. This referee cast the lone vote for challenger Jersey Joe Walcott in a hotly-disputed 1947 split-decision victory for Joe Louis. Name this courageous ref.
9. After awarding Tom Sharkey the match over Bob Fitzsimmons on a foul in the eighth round, referee ———————————— had to draw his six-gun to quell the angry mob who thought that Ruby Robert had landed a legitimate solar plexus blow.
10. Brought down from New York to referee the Young Stribling—Mike McTigue title fight in Columbus, Georgia, he first called the bout a draw, changed the verdict to a Stribling win under duress from both promoter and crowd, then later reverted to his original decision on a train heading back north. Who was this much-harried and maligned referee?
11. He ruled that Jack Sharkey's blow had struck Max Schmeling below the belt and awarded the heavyweight championship of the world to "The Black Uhlan."
12. Although referee Ollie Pecord counted champion Jess Willard out in the first round of his title fight with Jack Dempsey, the bout was allowed to continue for two more bloody rounds. Why did Willard receive this two-round reprieve?
13. In his second meeting with Cassius Clay, Sonny Liston was knocked down by a controversial "phantom punch" in the first round. Failing to realize that Liston had been on the canvas for ten seconds, the referee permitted Sonny to rise and continue the battle. Screaming at the top of his lungs from his ringside seat, *Ring* Editor Nat Fleischer convinced the referee that the fight should be stopped and Clay declared the winner by a knockout. Name the former heavyweight champion who came close to creating mass confusion in his handling of the referee's chores for this title fight.
14. *Third Man in the Ring* is the autobiography of referee ————————————.
15. This referee was forced to carry courageous Jimmy Wilde back to his corner when the little Welsh flyweight refused to concede defeat after suffering four 17th-round knockdowns at the hands of Pete Herman in their 1921 bout.

3. FIGHT SITES (15 pts)

Name the memorable bout which occurred at each of these storied sites.

1. Boyle's Thirty Acres, Jersey City, New Jersey (July 2, 1921)
2. Havana, Cuba (April 5, 1915)
3. Soldier's Field, Chicago, Illinois (September 22, 1927)
4. Maumee Bay, Toledo, Ohio (July 4, 1919)
5. Sydney, Australia (December 26, 1908)
6. Kingston, Jamaica (January 22, 1973)
7. Carson City, Nevada (March 17, 1897)
8. Shelby, Montana (July 4, 1923)

9. Reno, Nevada (July 4, 1910)
10. Kinshasa, Zaire (October 30, 1974)
11. Richburg, Mississippi (July 8, 1889)
12. Sesquicentennial Stadium, Philadelphia, Pennsylvania (September 23, 1926)
13. Olympic Club, New Orleans, Louisiana (September 7, 1892)
14. Long Island City, New York (June 13, 1935)
15. Caracas, Venezuela (March 26, 1974)

4. THE GREAT WHITE HOPES (10 pts.)

Angry whites tried to annoint a bogus heavyweight king when the first black champ was crowned. Try flying your colors on these "white hope" contenders.

1. The "Great White Hope" movement was a reaction against heavyweight champion _____.
2. Name the only "White Hope" to ever become champ.
3. Which French light-heavy claimed the "White Hope" title prior to his being defeated in an official heavyweight title match?
4. Name the red-haired "White Hope" who stung opponents with his powerful "Mary Ann" right-hand punch.
5. What "White Hope" contender worked as a plasterer?
6. What "White Hope" died in the ring at the tender age of twenty-one?
7. What "White Hope" was called "The Fireman?"
8. What "White Hope" fighter carried his anti-black feelings into a later career as a referee?
9. Who was the original "White Hope?"
10. Who won the "White Hope" Tournament in Los Angeles in 1913?

5. COUNTING FOR THE KNOCKDOWNS (10 pts.)

Try to beat the count on these exciting multiple-knockdown bouts.

1. What two boxers, one a future lightweight champ, participated in the 1902 bout which produced the most total knockdowns ever recorded in a single fight?
2. What two non-champs set the record for most total knockdowns in a single heavyweight bout?
3. Two boxers share the dubious honor of being knocked down the most times in one bout. Name these glass-jawed pugs.
4. Name the heavyweight who was knocked down the most times in one bout.
5. Name the "Iron Man" who was repeatedly knocked down—19 times by Jim Barry, 17 times by Bob Fitzsimmons, 15 times by Jack Johnson—but KO'd only three times in over 300 bouts.
6. What lightweight champ was involved in three bouts which produced more than ten knockdowns?
7. What championship bout yielded the most knockdowns?
8. What historic match-up resulted in the most knockdowns ever to be scored in a heavyweight title fight?

9. In what round of a heavyweight championship bout did the most total knockdowns occur?
10. What non-heavyweight championship contest set the record for most knockdowns in a single round?

6. THE FRIDAY-NIGHT FIGHTS (10 pts.)

How well do you remember the days when live boxing flourished as prime-time television entertainment?

1. What time did both the Wednesday and Friday-night fights go on the air?
2. Name the legendary New York Giant baseball announcer who provided the play-by-play on the Wednesday night fights.
3. Who replaced him at ringside in the late fifties?
4. Do you remember the now-famous psychologist who frequently appeared with him as a commentator on the Wednesday-night fights?
5. Who was the voice of the Friday-night fights?
6. Wavy-haired _____ the Bartender, hawked Pabst Blue Ribbon Beer between rounds on the Wednesday-night fights.
7. What was this familiar pitchman's full name?
8. ABC began broadcasting *The Fight of the Week* in 1960. Who handled the mike-side chores for these bouts?
9. On what day was *The Fight of the Week* telecast?
10. What shaving company sponsored NBC's Friday-night fights?

7. BELOW THE BELT (10 pts.)

Keep your punches up as you try to recall these errant blows which landed in foul territory.

1. Name the only fighter to win the heavyweight championship of the world while seated on the canvas.
2. Name the tough sailor who won by foul, over former heavyweight champs Bob Fitzsimmons and James J. Corbett.
3. Name the Panamanian fighter who was crowned lightweight champion when the referee refused titleholder Ken Buchanan's foul claim on the thirteenth round and awarded the knockout verdict to the challenger.
4. Benny Leonard lost his bid for the welterweight title when he was disqualified in the thirteenth round for hitting champion _____ when he was down.
5. Name the only heavyweight title fight in which the champion retained his crown via a foul disqualification.
6. What "Old Master" successfully defended his lightweight title when Battling Nelson was disqualified for striking a low blow in the forty-second round?
7. Who was awarded the light-heavyweight title on a sixth-round knockout when the French Boxing Federation reversed referee M. Bernstein's earlier disqualification of the challenger for tripping champion Georges Carpentier?
8. Who won the world lightweight title when champion Ad Wolgast was disqualified by referee Jim Griffin for deliberately fouling to avoid being knocked out?

9. What Olympic gold medal-winner won the undisputed welterweight championship of the world when Joe Dundee knocked him unconscious with a low blow?
10. Which one of the following champions did not win his world title on a foul? (a) Rube Ferns (b) Dixie Kid (c) Frank Klaus (d) Frankie Genaro (e) Marcel Thil (f) They all won their titles on fouls

8. EIGHT, NINE, TEN,—YER OUT! (10 pts.)

How many of these block-busting knockouts do you remember?

1. What former light-heavyweight champion did Joe Louis knock out in the first round of a 1939 title defense?
2. Tony Zale ended Rocky Graziano's brief one-year reign as middleweight champion by scoring a sensational knockout on a long left hook in the _____ round.
3. What controversial Argentinian middleweight became world champion by knocking out Italian glamour boy Nino Benvenuti in the twelfth round of their 1970 title match?
4. Floyd Patterson picked himself off the canvas twice in the first round to knock out Ingemar Johansson and write the final chapter in their financially-successful three-bout series. In what round did Floyd send Ingo crashing face first into boxing oblivion?
5. After winning and successfully defending his title against Mysterious Billy Smith, he lost his welterweight crown to Kid McCoy on a fifteenth round knockout in 1896. Name this double champion who won the middleweight crown two years after losing to McCoy.
6. Name the American fighter who won the light-heavyweight title on January 24, 1950 by knocking out Briton Freddie Mills in the tenth round of their championship tilt.
7. Who was the "Durable Dane" that Ad Wolgast knocked out in the fortieth round to capture the world lightweight championship?
8. Which of the following challengers did Joe Louis fail to kayo in a title defense? (a) Jack Roper (b) Bob Pastor (c) Johnny Paycheck (d) Harry Thomas (e) Red Burman
9. Who did N.B.A. lightweight king Ike Williams kayo to win recognition as undisputed world champion?
10. Name the "Tylerstown Terror" who became boxing's first flyweight champion by knocking out Young Zulu Kid in the eleventh round of their 1916 contest at London's Holborn Stadium.

9. BROTHER WARRIORS (10 pts.)

Match these famous fighters with their boxing brothers.

1. Terry McGovern   a. Phil, Marty and Monty
2. Abe Atell   b. Pete, Joe and Eddie
3. Leach Cross   c. Jose Luis and Fino
4. Fritzie Zivic   d. Monte and Caesar

5. Phil Terranova   e. Jack
6. Jesus Pimentel   f. Phil
7. Tommy Gibbons   g. Joe
8. Jerry Quarry   h. Mike J.
9. Vince Dundee   i. Mike
10. Mike Sullivan   j. Jack and Nat

10. MILLION DOLLAR GATES (10 pts.)

See if you can ring up these boxing bonanzas on your cash register.

1. What fight produced the first million dollar gate in boxing history?
2. What bout raked in the largest total of outdoor live-gate receipts?
3. What fight pulled in the largest total of indoor live-gate receipts?
4. What bout drew the largest outdoor attendance?
5. What bout brought out the largest indoor crowd?
6. What was the largest winning purse ever awarded to a fighter?
7. Including closed-circuit TV, what fight produced the largest all-time gate?
8. What heavyweight fought in three straight million dollar gates?
9. Five of Dempsey's last six bouts were million dollar gates. Name the only one which was a financial bust.
10. Name the only heavyweight champ besides Dempsey and Ali to repeatedly attract million dollar gates for his title fights.

11. RING ALIASES (15 pts.)

Identify these popular fighters from their real names.

1. Arnold Raymond Cream
2. Louis Phal
3. Albert Griffiths
4. Joe Barrow
5. Walker Smith, Jr.
6. Oscar Nielson
7. Henry Jackson
8. Joseph Paul Cukoschay
9. Sidney Walker
10. Joe de Melfi
11. Noah Brusso
12. Benjamin Leiner
13. Rocco Barbella
14. Jacob Finkelstein
15. Gershon Mendeloff

12. THE GREAT JOHN L. (10 pts.)

Put up your dukes and come to scratch against America's last bare-knuckle champion, the mighty John L. Sullivan.

1. What was the powerful John L.'s nickname?
2. What did the "L" stand for in Sullivan's middle name?
3. Who was the scientific boxing professor from Cincinnati that Sullivan chased around the ring for ten rounds before finally knocking him out in 1880?
4. Who did Sullivan knock out in nine rounds to capture the American bare-knuckle heavyweight championship (London Prize Ring rules)?
5. Although he managed to recover in time to win the three-round decision, Sullivan was knocked down for the first time in his career in the opening round by his most persistant ring nemesis. Name the crafty fighter who later employed a variety of ring tricks to earn a 39-round draw with Sullivan.
6. How many fights did Sullivan lose during his professional ring career? (a) 1   (b) 3   (c) 5   (d) 8   (e) 11
7. Although he suffered a broken arm during the fight, Sullivan weathered the storm to earn a draw against this leading heavyweight contender of the day. Who did John L. battle to a stalemate in this six-rounder fought in Minneapolis on January 18, 1887?
8. Sullivan locked horns with a formidable foe in a 75-round slugfest which lasted two hours and sixteen minutes. Who did the Irish-American champ finally stop in this 1887 fight-to-the-finish?
9. *True or False*: When James J. Corbett knocked out Sullivan in the twenty-first round of their 1892 title contest, it marked the first time gloves had been worn in a heavyweight championship fight.
10. Name John L.'s discipline-minded manager who often had to work long hard hours to get his fighter off the "sauce" and back into peak fighting condition.

13. GENTLEMAN JIM (10 pts.)

Climb into the ring and test yourself against master-boxer James J. Corbett, conqueror of the once-invincible John L. Sullivan.

1. What was Corbett's middle-class occupation before he embarked on a successful ring career?
2. What punch is Corbett credited with bringing to boxing?
3. Although Corbett fought most of the way with a broken thumb and several fractured knuckles in this 1889 bout, he still managed to knock out his smaller, worn-out opponent in the twenty-seventh round. Who was this kayo victim and bitter rival of Corbett both in and out of the ring?
4. Corbett toyed for six rounds with the man who had given John L. Sullivan the fight of his life only six months earlier. Name the great, bare-knuckle fighter who Corbett easily decisioned in this 1890 match.
5. Corbett defended his title on January 25, 1894 against Sullivan's old nemesis, Charley Mitchell. What was the outcome of their championship bout?
6. Who was Corbett's opponent when Edison's primitive kinetoscope recorded the first motion picture of a prize fight on September 7, 1894?

7. Who won this filmed six-round match?
8. In what round did Bob Fitzsimmons' solar plexus punch end Gentleman Jim's brief championship reign?
9. Jim came close to regaining his lost title when he fought recently-crowned champion James J. Jeffries on May 11, 1900. Corbett boxed rings around his slower-moving opponent until tagged by a knockout blow which dashed his hopes of reclaiming the heavyweight throne. In what round did the Boilermaker flatten Corbett?
10. What former welterweight champion did Corbett knock out in his last successful bout?

14. RUBY ROBERT (10 pts.)

Who could forget or deny the awesome punching power of "the fighting machine on stilts"—Bob Fitzsimmons?

1. *True or False*: Bob Fitzsimmons was the first triple champion in boxing history and one of only four men to accomplish this unique feat.
2. What three weight titles did "Ruby Robert" hold?
3. Who did "Freckled Bob" knock out in the thirteenth round to claim the middleweight championship of the world?
4. Name the tragic fighter who died after being knocked out by Fitz in the second round of their 1894 exhibition bout in Syracuse, New York.
5. After Corbett unofficially designated this Irishman as his successor, Fitzsimmons knocked him stiff in one minute and thirty-five seconds of the first round. Who did Bob kayo in this brief encounter, held in an outdoor ring pitched across the border from Langtry, Texas in Mexico on February 21, 1896?
6. How many times did Fitzsimmons successfully defend the heavyweight title he won from James J. Corbett on the much-publicized "solar plexus" punch?
7. *True or False*: Fitzsimmons was knocked out by four former world heavyweight champions during his ring career—Corbett, Jeffries, Burns, and Johnson.
8. On November 25, 1903, Fitzsimmons won his third and final world title by decisioning George Gardner over twenty rounds. Which weight division did Ruby Robert rule after this remarkable victory?
9. *True or False*: Bob Fitzsimmons was the first and only british-born fighter to hold the title of heavyweight champion of the world.
10. At which of Bob's major fights did wife Rosie exhort her spindle-legged husband to hit his opponent "in the slats?"

15. THE BOILERMAKER (10 pts.)

How well do you remember the rock-hard heavyweight champion James J. Jeffries and his uncanny ability to withstand brutal punishment while devastating opponents with his awesome punching power?

1. Jeffries engaged in fewer ring contests than any other man who held the heavyweight title. How many matches did Jeff wage: (a) 50 (b) 23 (c) 62 (d) 41 (e) 83?
2. After drawing with tough Gus Ruhlin over twenty gruelling rounds in his sixth

professional fight, Jeff next fought a bitterly-waged stalemate against a much smaller yet murderous-punching rival who had already extended Corbett twenty-seven rounds and drawn with Fitzsimmons. Who was this 160-pound mighty-mite?

3. Jeffries easily knocked out the shell of the once-feared "Black Prince" of boxing whom John L. Sullivan had repeatedly refused to fight during his reign as champion. Name the aging boxing-master Jeff kayoed in three rounds on March 22, 1898 in San Francisco.
4. Throwing everything but the kitchen sink at his young opponent, champion Bob Fitzsimmons finally fell victim to Jeffries' powerful right hand in their 1899 title fight. In what round did Jeff end the 37-year old Fitz's reign as heavyweight champion of the world?
5. Jeff narrowly escaped with his title in scoring a hard-fought 25-round decision in 1899 over an old rival he had outpointed the previous year. Name the rugged challenger who came close to dethroning the Boilermaker as heavyweight king.
6. *True or False*: Jeffries successfully defended his title by twice knocking out former champion James J. Corbett in the third round.
7. Who finally wrested the heavyweight title from Jeffries in late summer of 1904?
8. Jeff was coaxed out of retirement to carry the standard of the white race into the ring against the much-despised heavyweight champion Jack Johnson. How many rounds did Jeffries last against Li'l Arthur in their Reno, Nevada showdown on July 4, 1910?
9. How many times did Jeffries sink to the canvas during the final round of his losing effort against Jack Johnson?
10. *True or False*: The only loss Jeffries suffered in his entire professional career was at the hands of boxing stylist Jack Johnson in his unsuccessful bid to remove the "golden smile" from the "black bear's" face.

16. TINY TOMMY (10 pts.)

Do you remember when diminutive champ Tommy Burns was travelling around the world defending his heavyweight title?

1. Who did Burns decision over twenty rounds in winning the heavyweight championship of the world?
2. Who held Burns to a twenty-round draw in his second defense of the world title?
3. Which one of the following boxers did not engage Burns in a heavyweight title bout? (a) Philadelphia Jack O'Brien (b) Gunner Moir (c) Jewey Smith (d) Bill Lang (e) Joe Beckett
4. How many times did Tommy successfully defend his world title?
5. Name the persistent challenger Burns knocked out three times in separate title defenses.
6. Burns outpointed Philadelphia Jack O'Brien on May 8, 1907 in Los Angeles to retain his heavyweight crown. What other "unofficial" title did Tommy earn by his victory?
7. *True or False*: Tommy Burns was the shortest man to hold the world heavyweight title.
8. Which one of the following boxers did not defeat Burns during his career?: (a) Mike Shreck (b) Jack O'Brien (c) Jack Twin Sullivan (d) Hugo Kelly

12 / The World Championship Boxing Quizbook

9. *True or False*: Burns broke the color barrier for the first time in a heavyweight championship fight when he agreed to put his title on the line against cocky Jack Johnson.
10. *True or False*: Jack Johnson knocked Burns down and out in the fourteenth round on December 26, 1908 to win the heavyweight crown.

17. L'IL ARTHUR (10 pts.)

Do you remember the controversial reign of the world's first black heavyweight champion—Jack Johnson?

1. Johnson fought the immortal Sam Langford one time during his professional career. Who emerged as the victor in this vintage 1906 match between two of boxing's greatest black heavyweights?
2. *True or False*: Marvin Hart recovered from a first-round knockdown to eke out a twenty-round decision over Johnson on March 8, 1905 at San Francisco.
3. Name the 45-year old former heavyweight champion who Johnson retired in the second round of their 1907 tilt in Philadelphia.
4. Determined to capture the heavyweight title, Johnson pursued the reigning titleholder around the globe before finally cornering him in Sydney, Australia on December 26, 1908. Carrying the outclassed champion round after round to inflict bodily injury, Johnson appeared disappointed when police jumped into the ring to stop the carnage in the fourteenth round. Off whose head did Jack knock the heavyweight crown in this one-sided contest?
5. Jack was paired against the middleweight champion of the world in a 1909 title fight held at Colma, California. After suffering the embarrassment of a twelfth round knockdown, Johnson leaped to his feet, rushed across the ring, and pummeled his diminutive foe to the canvas. What was the name of L'il Arthur's wiry opponent in this topsy-turvy brawl?
6. How many times did Johnson defend his title before losing the crown to Willard?
7. Johnson deftly avoided his "Mary Ann" right-hand punch in carving out a twenty-round decision on June 27, 1914 in a Paris title bout. Who was this unsuccessful challenger to Jack's title?
8. Controversy shrouds Johnson's knockout defeat by colossus Jess Willard in the twenty-sixth round of their title fight in Havana, Cuba on April 5, 1915. Photographs show the fallen black champion lying prostrate on the canvas with his knees hunched up to avoid the hot floor and his arms shielding his eyes from the blinding sun. Jack claimed to have thrown the fight in exchange for amnesty from Federal charges pending against him. What statutory violation resulted in Johnson's serving one year in a Leavenworth jail?
9. Which of the following men did *not* defeat Jack Johnson in the prize ring? (a) Klondike (b) Joe Choynski (c) Joe Jeanette (d) Bearcat Wright (e) Sam McVey
10. Johnson was despised by whites for his amorous relationships with Caucasian women. How many white wives did Jack take during his controversial lifetime?

18. THE MANASSA MAULER (10 pts.)

Trace the career of the explosive, power-punching heavyweight legend, Jack Dempsey.

1. What ring name did Dempsey fight under during the early days of his career?
2. Strangely enough, Dempsey suffered two early career defeats at the hands of little-known Willie Meehan. Who was the only man to knock out the savage-punching Manassa Mauler?
3. Dempsey earned a title shot at champion Jess Willard by disposing of prominent heavyweight contenders Fred Fulton and Carl Morris in 1918. What was so unusual about the circumstances surrounding his kayo victories over both these men?
4. Outweighed by sixty pounds and giving away six inches in reach, Dempsey nevertheless all but destroyed hulking "Cowboy" Jess Willard in their 1919 title match. Jack bludgeoned the champion to the canvas seven times during the final minute of the opening round carnage in which Willard suffered a broken jaw, cracked ribs, and crushed cheekbones. After what round did the champion's corner throw in the towel to prevent their man from being killed?
5. How many rounds did it take Dempsey to dispose of the slender-built French "cream-puff" Georges Carpentier in their much-ballyhooed "Battle of the Century" on July 2, 1921?
6. Although hammered through the ropes onto a press reporter's typewriter during the first round, Dempsey recovered to knock out game challenger Louis Firpo in the anti-climactic second frame of their 1923 battle. How many times did Jack floor his brawling opponent in this never-to-be-forgotten ring war staged before 82,000 screaming fans at New York's Polo Grounds?
7. *True or False*: Dempsey successfully defended his title five times by knocking out Billy Miske, Bill Brennan, Georges Carpentier, Tommy Gibbons, and Luis Firpo before losing his crown to Gene Tunney by decision.
8. After losing his title to Gene Tunney in 1926, Dempsey earned a return match with the new titleholder by knocking out a future heavyweight champion in the seventh round of a 1927 elimination bout. Who did Dempsey kayo with a controversial short-chopping left hook?
9. Far behind on points during their second meeting, Dempsey finally caught up with the elusive champion Tunney with a five-punch flurry which sent the Fighting Marine sprawling to the canvas. Unfortunately for Jack, he failed to heed the referee's pre-fight instructions to proceed to the farthest neutral corner in the event of a knockdown. Tunney thus managed to struggle to his feet at the count of nine after being down an estimated fourteen seconds. In what round of the fight did this controversial "long count" occur?
10. While refereeing a wrestling match many years after hanging up his gloves, Jack was punched in the mouth by a publicity-seeking grappler. Pitted against the wrestler in a specially-arranged grudge match, Dempsey ended an eight-year ring absence by blasting his hopelessly out-classed opponent out of the ring and into a nearby hospital. Name Jack's inept foe in this farcical 1940 bout which was refereed by boxing historian Nat Fleischer.

14 / *The World Championship Boxing Quizbook*

19. THE FIGHTING MARINE (10 pts.)

Try your hand at answering these questions about the intellectual boxing-master Gene Tunney, perhaps best known for twice decisioning Jack Dempsey.

1. Who was the only man to defeat Tunney in a professional bout?
2. Who did Tunney outpoint over twelve rounds to win the American light-heavyweight championship?
3. Gene engaged in five brutal ring battles with tough middleweight Harry Greb. How did the Fighting Marine fare in his 5-bout series with his streetfighting foe?
4. *True or False*: Tunney regained the American light-heavyweight championship by knocking out Bill Brennan on February 23, 1923.
5. Jack Dempsey starched the "Orchid Man," Georges Carpentier, in four rounds at Boyle's Thirty Acres in 1921. How long did it take Gene to take out the French light-heavyweight when they clashed in the summer of 1924?
6. Although this crafty boxer lasted the full fifteen rounds in a losing effort against Jack Dempsey, Tunney was able to knock him out in the twelfth round. Who was this prominent heavyweight contender?
7. How many times did Tunney defend his heavyweight title?
8. *True or False*: Tunney fought Dempsey in a driving rain during their second meeting in which Gene weathered the "long count" knockdown to retain the heavyweight title.
9. *True or False*: After beating the "long count" in his rematch with former champion Jack Dempsey, Gene recovered to batter the weary Manassa Mauler to the canvas in the following round.
10. Who was the New Zealander Tunney stopped in the eleventh round at New York's Polo Grounds on July 26, 1928 in his final bout before retiring as undefeated heavyweight champion of the world at age thirty.

20. THE BOSTON GOB (10 pts.)

Take a jab at these brain-teasing questions about the erratic and high-strung Jack Sharkey.

1. Although Dempsey allegedly ducked a match with Harry Wills, Sharkey took on the feared Negro heavyweight on October 12, 1926 at Brooklyn, New York. How did Jack fare against this powerfully-built 212-pounder?
2. Name the former light-heavyweight champion who Sharkey knocked out cold in the first round of an April 30, 1928 bout at Madison Square Garden.
3. Match Sharkey's opponent with his performance in the ring against Jack.

    (1) Tom Heeney   (a) Lost decision 10, 7Won decision 15
    (2) Young Stribling   (b) Lost decision 10
    (3) Johnny Risko   (c) Won decision 10
    (4) Tommy Loughran   (d) Draw 12
    (5) King Levinsky   (e) KO'd in 3, Won decision 15

4. When Gene Tunney retired from the ring as undefeated heavyweight champion of the world, Sharkey was matched against Max Schmeling to determine a successor to the vacant throne. In what round did Sharkey foul Schmeling with a controversial low blow and temporarily forfeit his chances of becoming world champ?

5. *True or False*: Sharkey easily outpointed Primo Carnera in a lopsided fifteen-round points decision October 12, 1931.
6. After successfully defending his title against Young Stribling in Cleveland, Max Schmeling gave Sharkey a shot at his heavyweight crown. Jack responded by besting the German champion in yet another controversial fight. How did Sharkey defeat "Herr Max" to win the world heavyweight title?
7. How many times did Sharkey successfully defend his heavyweight title?
8. Who knocked out Sharkey in the sixth round on June 29, 1933 to win the heavyweight championship of the world?
9. What type of punch did Jack's clumsy opponent use to kayo him in this title match?
10. Who ended Sharkey's career by knocking him out in three furious rounds?

21. THE LIVERMORE LARRUPER (10 pts.)

Do you remember the ring antics of Max Baer, the "Clown Prince" of boxing?

1. Although Ernie Schaaf died of brain injuries after being KO'd by Primo Carnera in thirteen rounds, most boxing experts felt that he had finally succumbed to the ferocious beating he absorbed in his losing effort against Max Baer six months earlier. Name another up-and-coming heavyweight who died in late summer of 1930 after being knocked out by Baer in the fifth round.
2. Which one of the following men did not defeat Max Baer at some point in his checkered career? (a) Ernie Schaaf (b) Johnny Risko (c) Tommy Loughran (d) Tom Heeney (e) Les Kennedy
3. Name the rock-hard Basque who defeated Max over twenty rounds on July 4, 1931 in Reno, Nevada.
4. Max bombarded this former heavyweight king with powerful right-hand blows to the head in the tenth round of their 1933 bout to earn both a TKO victory and a shot at the world title. What ex-champ did Baer beat into submission on this June evening in New York?
5. What insignia did Baer have stitched onto his boxing trunks?
6. What inept titleholder did Max stop in eleven rounds to claim the heavyweight championship of the world?
7. How many times did Baer successfully defend his title?
8. Max's clowning finally caught up with him on the night of June 13, 1935 when he defended his title against journeyman James J. Braddock. How did Baer lose his title to the "Cinderella Man?" (a) TKO 6 (b) KO 4 (c) Decision 15 (d) KO 12 (e) TKO 9
9. What light-heavyweight resorted to hypnosis to knock out Baer in eight rounds in Max's final appearance in a professional prize ring?
10. Max's son starred in a popular CBS comedy series. Do you remember the role Junior created in this long-running rural sitcom?

22. THE BROWN BOMBER (13 pts.)

Let's revisit the days when the world's perfect fighting machine, Joe Louis, reigned supreme as king of the heavies.

16 / The World Championship Boxing Quizbook

1. Which former heavyweight champ did Louis fight in his first major bout after rolling up an impressive string of 22 wins (18 by KO) in less than a year as a pro?
2. Who did Louis knock out in the eighth round in Chicago's Comiskey Park on June 27, 1937 to become the first black heavyweight champion since Jack Johnson?
3. What was so unusual about the financial arrangements which were made for this bout?
4. *True or False*: Louis fought eight former heavyweight champs before hanging up his gloves for the last time in 1951.
5. What was the name of the skillful Welsh boxer whom Louis outpointed in his first defense of the heavyweight title in August, 1937?
6. Al McCoy, Red Burman, Gus Dorazio, Abe Simon, Tony Musto, and Buddy Baer were all members of an exclusive "club" which Louis defended his title against over a six-month period. What did the press call this hopelessly outclassed collection of "challengers" to Louis' title?
7. How long did it take an emotionally-charged up Louis to avenge his earlier knockout defeat at the fists of the bushy-browed German Max Schmeling in their 1938 title rematch?
8. Who lasted longer in the ring with Louis—former heavyweight champion Max Baer or his ponderous younger brother, Buddy?
9. Louis was floored eight times during his professional career. Name each fighter who scored a knockdown against this boxing immortal.
10. What political candidate did Louis tour the country for in 1940?
11. Who did Louis knock out in eleven rounds on June 25, 1948 in his last title defense before retiring as undefeated world heavyweight champion the following year?
12. Joe reigned as heavyweight king for a record eleven years before retiring as undefeated world champion on March 1, 1949. How many times did Louis successfully defend his title during this period?
13. How many fights did Joe lose during his spectacular 18-year ring career?

23. THE BROCKTON BLOCKBUSTER (10 pts.)

Do you remember the stocky, wade-in bruiser with the sledgehammer fists and granite jaw—Rocky Marciano?

1. How many of Marciano's forty-nine professional fights ended in a knockout? (a) 47 (b) 25 (c) 43 (d) 35 (e) 20
2. *True or False*: Rocky Marciano is the only heavyweight champion of the world never to have tasted defeat in professional competition.
3. Rocky fought a rather flabby, over-the-hill Joe Louis a year before winning the heavyweight title. How many rounds did it take the young bull Marciano to knock out the shell of the former great "Brown Bomber?"
4. Marciano picked himself off the canvas in the first round to battle his way back to a knockout victory over champion Jersey Joe Walcott at Philadelphia on September 23, 1952. In what round did Rocky tag Jersey Joe with a bone-crunching right to the jaw to end the latter's brief reign as heavyweight king?
5. How long did it take Marciano to take out Walcott in their May 15, 1953 rematch in Chicago?

6. *True or False*: Ezzard Charles fell victim to Rocky's knockout punch in two 1954 title fights.
7. How many times did Rocky successfully defend his heavyweight crown?
8. What cunning light-heavyweight champion did Marciano flatten in nine rounds in his final defense of his heavyweight title?
9. How many times was Marciano knocked down in his professional career?
10. Name the Negro fighter who handed Rocky his only defeat as an amateur.

24. THE RABBIT (10 pts.)

Who could forget the humble, glass-jawed heavyweight champ, Floyd Patterson—who once went so far as to pick up opponent Charley Polite from the canvas after knocking him down!

1. *True or False*: Floyd Patterson became the youngest man to win the heavyweight championship of the world when he flattened "Ancient" Archie Moore in five rounds on November 30, 1956 at the tender age of twenty-one.
2. How many times was Patterson knocked down in his career?
3. After winning an elimination bout against Archie Moore to determine Rocky Marciano's successor, Floyd successfully defended his crown against a quartet of mediocre opponents, including Hurricane Jackson, Roy Harris, and Brian London. Who did Patterson knock out in his lone title defense during his second reign as champion?
4. Floyd lost his title for the first time on June 26, 1959 when his jaw ran into Ingemar Johansson's "Hammer of Thor." How many times did the handsome Swede drop Patterson in the third round before referee Ruby Goldstein stepped in to halt the lopsided contest?
5. Name the Olympic gold medal-winner who fought Patterson for the heavyweight title in his first professional bout.
6. Patterson became the first man to regain the heavyweight championship when he leveled Ingemar Johansson with a sweeping left hook in their June 20, 1960 rematch. In what round did "The Rabbit" deliver the coup-de-grace to Ingo's chin?
7. *True or False*: Patterson survived two first round knockdowns to register a sixth-round kayo victory over challenger Ingemar Johansson in the rubber match of their three-fight series.
8. "Mr. Nice Guy" lost the heavyweight title for the second time when menacing Sonny Liston punched Floyd out with child-like ease in 2:06 seconds of the first round in their 1962 title fight. What happened in their July rematch the following year?
9. Name the W.B.A. heavyweight champion who "won" a controversial fifteen-round decision over Patterson before an angered Swedish audience in Stockholm on September 14, 1968.
10. Who tagged Patterson with the nickname "The Rabbit" prior to his scoring two TKO victories over Floyd?

18 / The World Championship Boxing Quizbook

25. THE UGLY BEAR (10 pts.)

Do you remember when menacing-looking, ex-convict Sonny Liston was knocking opponents stiff with his sledgehammer punches?

1. What was Sonny's real first name?
2. Liston absorbed his first loss when he suffered a broken jaw in his eighth professional fight. Refusing to concede defeat, however, Sonny plugged away for six more rounds before losing on points. Who was the Detroit veteran that busted up the up-and-coming Liston in 1954?
3. Liston twice crushed this Texas "Big Cat" on second and third-round knockouts. Name the victim of Sonny's angry fists who was later shot in the stomach by a police officer while resisting arrest.
4. Which one of the following heavyweight contenders escaped Liston's knockout punch? (a) Wayne Bethea (b) Mike De John (c) Roy Harris (d) Zora Folley (e) Eddie Machen
5. What fighter disdainfully referred to Liston as "the ugly bear?"
6. *True or False*: Liston whipped Floyd Patterson in a pair of first-round knockouts to win, then retain, the heavyweight title.
7. Why did Sonny quit on his stool and refuse to come out for the seventh round against brash Cassius Clay?
8. In what round did Liston fall to Ali's "invisible punch" during their May 25, 1965 rematch in Lewiston, Maine?
9. Who is the only man, aside from Muhammad Ali, to have knocked out the powerful-punching Liston?
10. Liston kayoed "the Bayonne Bleeder" in the tenth round of his final fight. Name this bartender-pugilist who was stopped in fifteen rounds by Muhammad Ali in the latter's first defense of his second reign as world champion.

26. SMOKIN' JOE 10 pts.)

Who will ever forget the relentless headhunter with the vicious left hook and lion-hearted courage—Joe Frazier?

1. What was the name of the corporation that "bought" Joe Frazier during the early days of his professional boxing career?
2. Joe recovered from two second-round knockdowns to outpoint this Argentinian brawler in a rough-and-tumble 1966 bout at Madison Square Garden. Name this South American mauler who Frazier later decisioned over fifteen rounds in a 1968 title defense.
3. Joe became the first man to stop this leading Canadian heavyweight contender by scoring a sensational TKO in the fourth round. Name this wade-in puncher who bled profusely under Joe's unrelenting attack in their 1967 encounter.
4. After Ali had been stripped of his title for refusing induction into the Armed Forces, Joe was matched against a blubbery 243-pound foe who was responsible for his lone defeat as an amateur. Name "The Blimp" who Joe smoked in two minutes and 33 seconds of the eleventh round on March 4, 1968 to win recognition as the N.B.A. heavyweight champ.

5. *True or False*: Frazier scored close decisions over Irish Jerry Quarry in both 1969 and 1974.
6. Name the light-punching W.B.A. champion Joe destroyed in five short rounds with his powerhouse left hook to claim the undisputed heavyweight championship of the world.
7. What light-heavyweight champion was kayoed in two rounds by Joe in a 1970 title defense?
8. In one of the greatest upsets in boxing history, Frazier lost his world title to powerful George Foreman on a two-round TKO. How many times did Joe hit the canvas in this one-sided beating?
9. After splitting their first two meetings, Ali and Frazier locked horns in the rubber match which many boxing enthusiasts regard as one of the greatest heavyweight bouts of all time. In what round did the nimble-footed Ali finally stop Smokin' Joe?
10. How many knockdowns occurred in Joe's three-fight series with Muhammad Ali?

27. PUGILISTIC POTPOURRI (20 pts.)

Find the names of the twenty boxing celebrities hidden in this square of alphabet jibberish.

```
B A D E G L O O Z N I R T E L J U T R E E M O P J
E K O I G O R O S S U F I D E W X V O L K Y U K O
P L O G R U I J E F X W I N D O N E R O M E G G Y
O R D E H I C H O P P I Y A S T L D O L E Q U I G
T R Y I J O K O U Z A L E T R U K I O O S P U G H
H I K I M W A T T R E L O P L U D L E X U V E T Y
O U J I P A R E T Y E S H U T R O L I B L I F F O
Y I C K E D D O O F E G R I Q U N O J E L E E V S
I R F O J E R B L E S K I C A L I N U T I M E S T
P Y R I H E D D O L P E X E C R I G K O V E S K Y
O F E W A L C O T T I D E M I X I F O Z A T E N W
R E P L O J E D I G H T C O R B E T T I N O O K E
U N G E U D O R P E M O L L U J E Q U O G O M M I
D E P O H U C R A V E D I K L O S S E W I B O V E
R I A L E N O O S T I C O P R I H E Q X O L L U M
I D P R O D E T T E C O S E L L E L O G G E W A X
J I K U R E F O R E M A N I J O R I S S I G L I B
I P E T T E D L A R T O K S T R I B L I N G E P U
W I F O O L O N N I K E F O H I C K O M E Z I J E
O G U K E M C C O Y E D D I G O L E M I W U F F O
P R I H O L L D E S H O M F P R I T U N N E Y I X
O F R A Z I E R O O H E D I J O N N E F I Q U A B
L I F L A D E Y O K O B B E W G H I R Y O P E G G
O D E H I K K O S E T R I N O R T O N E S F I L E
Q U O L E G G O U S H E T H O M M E W A F U G R E
```

QUESTIONS / 21

28. IN THIS CORNER.... PHOTO QUIZ I (10 pts.)

How many of these former boxing champions can you identify?

1. Light-heavyweight champion
June 25, 1930—November 16, 1934

22 / The World Championship Boxing Quizbook

2. Lightweight champion
August 24, 1956—April 21, 1962

QUESTIONS / 23

3. Heavyweight champion
June 12, 1930—June 21, 1932

24 / *The World Championship Boxing Quizbook*

**4. Middleweight champion
July 16, 1947—June 10, 1948**

QUESTIONS / 25

**5. Heavyweight champion
December 26, 1908—April 5, 1915**

26 / *The World Championship Boxing Quizbook*

**6. Lightweight champion
May 28, 1917—1925 (retired)**

7. Light-heavyweight champion
October 12, 1920—September 24, 1922

8. Middleweight champion
July 19, 1940—July 16, 1947
and
June 10, 1948—September 21, 1948

QUESTIONS / 29

9. Bantamweight champion
   September 12, 1899—early 1900 (vacated title)
      and
   Featherweight champion
   January 9, 1900—November 28, 1901

30 / *The World Championship Boxing Quizbook*

**10. Heavyweight champion
July 3, 1905—February 23, 1906**

29. BARE-KNUCKLES (15 pts.)

Match up these old-timers with their claim to fame during the early years when opponents boxed without gloves in the mud.

1. Daniel Mendoza
2. Tom Hyer, son of Jacob Hyer
3. John L. Sullivan
4. Jem Mace
5. Jacob Hyer beat Tom Beasley
6. Jake Kilrain
7. Jack Broughton
8. James Figg
9. John Morrissey
10. Arthur Chambers
11. Tom Cribb
12. Paddy Ryan
13. Tom Molineaux
14. "Bendigo" (William Thompson)

a. Father of boxing, drew up first rules
b. First heavyweight champion
c. First scientific boxer
d. Lost in last bareknuckle championship fight
e. Won in last bareknuckle championship fight
f. First American heavyweight champ
g. Heavyweight champ who taught modern scientific boxing
h. First great lightweight
i. Early American heavyweight champ, served two terms in Congress
j. Stopped by John L. Sullivan in nine rounds
k. Sleeping lion memorial tombstone in Nottingham
l. First ring contest in America
m. First international title bout
n. Celebrated Britisher who beat Molineaux
o. First major American black boxer, fought mainly in England

30. RULES OF THE GAME (10 pts.)

Can you match up these evolutionary changes in the sport of boxing?

1. Authorized 15-round decison bouts, set up modern commissions
2. Compulsory 8-count on knockdowns
3. Boxer can't be saved by the bell if knocked down
4. Allowed 30 seconds to come to "scratch" with corner's assistance in rough bouts of unlimited rounds
5. Permitted referee decisions and no round limits for bouts
6. Established gloved bouts, 3-minute rounds with one minute rest between, ten seconds to get up unassisted, and prohibited wrestling
7. Adopted three-knockdown rule
8. Permitted ten-round no decision bouts, set up first commission
9. Protective cup prevented loss of bouts from low blows
10. Eliminated liquor from corner's "water" bottle, expanded list of foul violations

a. New York (1965)
b. Broughton Rules (1743)
c. Houtin Law, New York (1886-1900)
d. London Prize Ring Rules (1838)
e. New York (1957)
f. Walker Law, New York (1920)
g. New York (1951)
h. Frawley Law, New York (1911-1917)
i. New York (1930)
j. Marquess of Queensberry Rules (1867)

31. THE DOUGHBOYS RETURN (10 pts.)

Match these boxers with the branch of the Armed Forces in which they served.

1. Rocky Marciano
2. Gunboat Smith
3. Sam Collyer
4. Terry Downes
5. Ken Overlin
6. Marcel Cerdan
7. Randy Turpin
8. Abe Brown
9. Harold Dade
10. Bob Foster

a. U.S. Navy
b. Inter-Allied middleweight champ
c. U.S. Marines
d. All-Service lightweight champ
e. U.S. Air Force
f. U.S. Army
g. Britisher in U.S. Marines
h. U.S. Navy, after Spanish-American War
i British Army
j. Union Army, won Congressional Medal of Honor

32. GOING THE DISTANCE (10 pts.)

How many of these classic decision bouts do you remember?

1. Who won, lost, and regained his welterweight title on a series of three fifteen-round decision bouts with Jimmy McLarnin?
2. *True or False*: Sugar Ray Robinson lost four world middleweight titles on fifteen-round decisions to Randy Turpin, Gene Fullmer, Carmen Basilio, and Bobo Olson.
3. Who ended Abe Attell's ten-year reign as featherweight champ with a twenty-round decision over him on February 22, 1912 at Vernon, California?
4. Which one of triple-champ Henry Armstrong's three world titles did he not win by decision?
5. Which one of the following heavyweights did not go the distance in his fight(s) with Muhammad Ali? (a) Joe Bugner (b) Ernie Terrell (c) George Chuvalo (d) Buster Mathis (e) Oscar Bonavena
6. Who was the only man to last the full fifteen rounds in a heavyweight title fight with Rocky Marciano?
7. Who began his nine-year rule as light-heavy king with a fifteen-round points decision over Joey Maxim on December 17, 1952 at St. Louis?
8. *True or False*: Primo Carnera's only two successful defenses of his heavyweight crown came on fifteen-round decisions over Paolino Uzcudun and Johnny Risko.
9. Name the feared "Giant-Killer" Battling Levinsky decisioned over twelve rounds on October 24, 1916 to win the light-heavyweight title.
10. Name the local boy who outslugged and outboxed welterweight champion Mickey Walker over ten rounds to win the title before 13,000 disbelieving hometown fans.

33. WE WUZ ROBBED! (10 pts.)

The official decision may not always be the "right" one—at least not to the loser. How many of these ring controversies do you remember?

1. Who was the only fighter to win the heavyweight title on a foul?
2. Who won the rematch after which the mayor of New York apologized for the controversial decision?
3. Who decisioned Joe Louis (according to referee Ruby Goldstein) but lost the fight when both judges disagreed?
4. Who lost his title by a close decision when the referee took five rounds away from him for fouling?
5. When was Willie Pep twice wrong as a referee?
6. Who beat Jack Johnson under very strange circumstances?
7. What French middleweight won three title bouts in Paris on fouls?
8. How was Ray Robinson robbed of a clear KO victory in Berlin?
9. Who robbed Robinson twice in Boston?
10. Who "stole" a title from the little Welshman Jimmy Wilde in London?

34. TALE OF THE TAPE (10 pts.)

How many of these former heavyweight champions can you identify from their vital statistics?

	1	2	3	4	5
Height:	5'7"	5'11¾	6'5¾"	6'3"	6'6¼"
Weight:	170 lbs.	167-176 lbs.	267 lbs.	212 lbs.	250 lbs.
Reach:	74½ in.	71¾ in.	85½½ in.	80 in.	83 in.
Chest:	40 in.	41 in.	48 in.	43 in.	46 in.
Chest (Exp):	44 in.	44 in.	54 in.	45 in.	49½ in.
Waist:	33 in.	32 in.	38 in.	34 in.	35½ in.
Biceps:	14½ in.	12 in.	18½ in.	15 in.	17½ in.
Neck:	16 in.	15 in.	20 in.	17½ in.	17½ in.
Wrist:	7¼ in.	7½ in.	9½ in.	8 in.	10 in.
Calf:	16½ in.	13½ in.	20 in.	17 in.	17½ in.
Ankle:	8¼ in.	8¼ in.	11½ in.	9½ in.	10½ in.
Thigh:	22 in.	20 in.	30 in.	26 in.	26 in.
Fist:	12 in.	12½ in.	15 in.	13 in.	14 in.
Forearm:	13 in.	11½ in.	16 in.	13½ in.	14 in.

	6	7	8	9	10
Height:	6'	5'10"	6'1"	5'11"	6'¼"
Weight:	182 lbs.	200 lbs.	190 lbs.	185 lbs.	220 lbs.
Reach:	71 in.	74 in.	77 in.	68 in.	74 in.
Chest:	40 in.	44½ in.	42 in.	39 in.	37½ in.
Chest (Exp.)	42 in.	46½ in.	46 in.	42 in.	42½ in.
Waist:	32½ in.	38½ in.	33 in.	32 in.	36 in.
Biceps:	14½ in.	15 in.	16¼ in.	14 in.	16 in.
Neck:	16½ in.	16½ in.	17 in.	16¾ in.	17½ in.
Wrist:	6 in.	8 in.	9 in.	7½ in.	10½ in.
Calf:	15½ in.	16 in.	15 in.	14¾ in.	15 in.
Ankle:	9½ in.	9½ in.	9 in.	10 in.	Not Available
Thigh:	21½ in.	25 in.	23 in.	22 in.	22½ in.
Fist:	12½ in.	13½ in.	11¼ in.	11½ in.	14 in.
Forearm:	12 in.	13 in.	14½ in.	12 in.	14½ in.

35. BOXING PECULIARITIES (10 pts.)

Can you match these boxers with their tell-tale ring traits?

1. Battling Nelson
2. Sugar Ray Robinson
3. Ad Wolgast
4. Leach Cross
5. Beau Jack
6. Johnny Dundee
7. Billy Conn
8. George Chuvalo
9. Joey Giardello
10. Jimmy McLarnin

a. Defensive shell of arms and elbows
b. Would bound off the ropes
c. Eyes cut easily
d. Skillfull in contract negotiations
e. Could not be knocked down
f. Bolo puncher
g. Fared better in long bouts
h. Did handsprings after scoring knockdown
i. Suffered fifteen bone breaks
j. Hotheaded

36. THE NEAR-CHAMPS (10 pts.)

Some boxers came within an eyelash of winning the title. Can you pull these answers out?

1. He knocked champion Jack Jeffries down and may have out-pointed him in a four-round exhibition bout.
2. Although he was forced to quit with a broken hand, Jack Johnson was awarded a draw in this ten-round Paris title bout. What fighter was robbed of a TKO victory?
3. Before losing his title to Fitzsimmons, Corbett prematurely announced his retirement and "bestowed" the title to this fighter.
4. The W.B.A. gave the title to this man when Muhammad Ali adopted his Muslim name after beating Liston.

5. This black boxer fought a 61-round draw with Corbett and would have beaten Sullivan (whom Corbett won the title from) had he been given the chance to fight him.
6. He fought a three-round draw with Sullivan and lost a close 25-round decision to Jeffries.
7. This light-heavyweight stopped Fitzsimmons in thirteen rounds after Fitz had lost the title, and lost a twenty-round decision to Tommy Burns in a bout which was dead-even.
8. He was leading in rounds when stopped by Marvin Hart in the twelfth frame of the elimination bout to crown Jeffries' successor.
9. If he had claimed foul after Jack Dempsey was helped back into the ring by sportswriters in the press row, he would probably have been declared champion.
10. He led Ali in rounds until the referee stopped the bout in the eleventh round and awarded Ali the TKO victory.

37. TINSEL TOWN BOXERS (10 pts.)

Let's reminisce about the ketsup-laced bouts which were staged in Hollywood arenas throughout moviedom.

1. Who was the only Oscar-winning actor to vie for the heavyweight championship of the world?
2. Who starred as former middleweight champ Rocky Graziano in the autobiographical film *Somebody Up There Likes Me?*
3. What celebrated comedian once fought under the ring name of Packy East?
4. What actor portrayed the title role in the *The Joe Louis Story?*
5. Who starred as broken-down prize fighter Mountain McClintock in Rod Serling's original teleplay *Requiem for a Heavyweight,* originally broadcast as the second installment of *Playhouse 90* on October 11, 1956?
6. What was the name of the 1949 film in which Kirk Douglas created the memorable role of unscrupulous fighter Midge Kelly?
7. Name the dashing adventure-film star who played the role of James J. Corbett, second modern heavyweight champion of the world, in *Gentleman Jim.*
8. What was the name of the Broadway stage actor who delivered a virtuoso performance as black champion Jack Jefferson (Johnson) in the stage play and film version of *The Great White Hope?*
9. The hard-hitting boxing film, *The Harder They Fall,* was loosely based upon the life of what immigrant heavyweight champion?
10. Aside from battling his way to the welterweight championship of the world, Barney Ross waged a victorious campaign over his addiction to narcotic drugs. What was the name of the Hollywood production which told the gripping tale of Ross' triumphs both in and outside of the ring?

38. NICKNAMES I (15 pts.)

Can you identify these boxing champions from their colorful nicknames?

1. The Pittsburgh Windmill
2. Gunboat
3. The Nebraska Wildcat
4. Will-o'-the-Wisp
5. The Orchid Man
6. Bummy
7. The Toy Bulldog
8. Little Chocolate
9. Two Ton
10. The Fargo Express
11. The Cinderella Man
12. Ghost with a Hammer in his Hand
13. The Bronx Bull
14. Old Bones
15. The Herkimer Hurricane

39. NICKNAMES II (10 pts.)

Round two—match the boxer with his ring monicker.

1. Bombardier
2. The Cincinnati Cobra
3. The Wild Bull of the Pampas
4. Baby Face
5. The Georgia Deacon
6. Philadelphia
7. Homicide Hank
8. The Hawaiian Swede
9. Cannonball
10. The Pittsburgh Kid

a. Tiger Flowers
b. Louis Angel Firpo
c. Carl Bobo Olson
d. Billy Conn
e. Ezzard Charles
f. Billy Wells
g. Jack O'Brien
h. Eddie Martin
i. Jimmy McLarnin
j. Henry Armstrong

40. FIGHT LINGO (10 pts.)

Tell it like it is—well almost! Can you decipher these boxing terms?

1. Palooka
2. Swings like a gate
3. Nobber
4. Annie Oakley
5. A lallapalooza
6. Horizontal fighter
7. Claret
8. Mill
9. Like a washer woman
10. A teaser

41. THE MICHIGAN ASSASSIN (10 pts.)

Step into the ring and go a few rounds with the all-time middleweight champ Stanley Ketchel.

1. What was Ketchel's real name?
2. Although he hailed from Grand Rapids, Michigan, Ketchel did most of his early fighting in _____.
3. Ketchel claimed the title after scoring a 32-round KO victory over _____.
4. Ketchel gained universal title acclaim after blasting out _____ in the first round.
5. What relative of the previous opponent did Ketchel defeat in his next bout?
6. Under what circumstances did Ketchel temporarily lose his title?
7. How long did Ketchel recuperate before winning the title back?
8. What was the result of Ketchel's fourth and final bout with Billy Papke?
9. Ketchel stepped up to the light-heavy class and twice defeated champion _____.
10. Although Jack Johnson promised to carry Ketchel the distance in their title fight, the bout ended abruptly in a twelfth-round KO victory for Johnson. What happened to change the pre-fight arrangements?

42. MAMA'S BOY (10 pts.)

Watch out for deceptive feinting and distractive ring chatter as you try to solve the slick-boxing style of lovable Benny Leonard.

1. Who did Leonard knock out in nine rounds on May 28, 1917 to win the lightweight championship of the world?
2. How many times did Benny successfully defend his world title?
3. *True or False*: Jimmy Goodrich stopped Leonard in the eleventh round of their 1924 title bout to win the world lightweight championship.
4. How many fights did this boxing master lose during his professional ring career? (a) none (b) 5 (c) 10 (d) 20 (e) 32
5. How many years did Leonard reign as king of the lightweight division?
6. Which one of the following boxers did not compete against Leonard in a lightweight title bout? (a) Rocky Kansas (b) Phil Bloom (c) Charley White (d) Richie Mitchell (e) Johnny Kilbane
7. Name the former world featherweight champion who fought eight no-decision bouts with Leonard.
8. Although staggered and grievously hurt in the eighth round, Leonard used his ring savvy to recover his senses and retain his title in this 1922 no-decision bout fought at Boyle's Thirty Acres. Name the rugged Jewish southpaw who came close to dethroning Leonard as lightweight champion in this epic fight.
9. After battering his opponent to the canvas three times during the opening round, Leonard was shocked by a left-right combination which dumped him to the floor before the gong had sounded to end the first three minutes of fighting. Name the game challenger who Leonard finally kayoed in the sixth round to retain his world title.
10. What former welterweight champion stopped Leonard the in the sixth round on October 7, 1932 to end Benny's illustrious ring career?

43. SUGAR RAY (10 pts.)

How well do you remember the boxing exploits of the man who was acclaimed by many as being the best "pound-for-pound" fighter in boxing history?

1. Robinson fought successfully as an amateur under his real name. What was it?
2. Robinson's first professional bout at age 20 was on the undercard the night Armstrong lost his welterweight title to Fritzie Zivic (October 4, 1940). Where did he make his debut?
3. By July 21, 1941 (after less than a year as a pro) Robinson had won all 21 of his bouts (17 by KO), beaten the reigning champ in a non-title bout, and been labeled the uncrowned champ in the _____ division.
4. What title did Robinson hold without a defeat for four years before becoming middleweight champ?
5. By winning his first middleweight title on February 17, 1951, Robinson avenged his only loss in his first eleven years as a pro. Who did he beat?
6. How many times did Robinson hold the middleweight title?
7. Robinson was stopped only one time in 202 bouts. By who?
8. On three separate occasions, Robinson lost his title and regained it in a return match. Name his opponent in each of these bouts.
9. Who is the only man to win the title from Robinson and successfully defend it in a return match?
10. Robinson boxed ten more years from 1955-1965 after coming out of retirement. Did he compile a winning record in the title bouts he engaged in during that period?

44. THE OLD MONGOOSE (12 pts.)

Do you remember when "Ageless" Archie Moore was knocking opponents stiff when most men his age were playing with their grandchildren?

1. How many times did Archie fight for the heavyweight championship of the world?
2. Name Moore's ring-wise manager who had already gained worldwide recognition for guiding a former world heavyweight champion to boxing's richest prize.
3. When Moore was hurt during a fight, he covered up his stomach and chin in an unorthodox defensive posture which he called the "_____."
4. What former heavyweight champion twice decisioned Moore over ten frames and kayoed the "Old Mongoose" in the eighth round of their third meeting on January 13, 1948?
5. How many professional fights did Moore have under his belt before he fought for the light-heavyweight title? (a) 30 (b) 80 (c) 110 (d) 170 (e) 230
6. How many times did Moore successfully defend his light-heavyweight crown?
7. *True or False*: Joey Maxim and Giulio Rinaldo are the only two challengers to go the distance with Moore in a title fight.
8. After being flattened three times in the first round and once in the fifth, Moore fought back to knock out French-Canadian underdog _____ in the eleventh round of their topsy-turvy 1958 title fight.
9. How did the forty-nine year old Moore fare against Cassius Clay when they met fifteen months before "The Louisville Lip" won the heavyweight championship of the world?

10. Name the reigning middleweight champion who Moore knocked out in the third round of a 1955 defense of his light-heavy crown.
11. The Ageless Wonder came within a whisker of dethroning Rocky Marciano as world heavyweight champion when he knocked the Rock down with a murderous right uppercut in the second round of their 1955 bout. Much to Moore's surprise, Marciano rose at the count of "three" and proceeded to gradually deflate Archie's hopes for the heavyweight title. In what round did Marciano eventually knock out the tiring Moore with a blistering attack?
12. Who did Moore lose the light-heavyweight title to in 1962?

45. THE BOSTON TAR BABY (10 pts.)

Sam Langford was perhaps the best heavyweight who never won the title. Take your best shots at these questions about his career.

1. Why was Langford called the "Boston Tar Baby?"
2. Langford fought in every division from lightweight through heavyweight from 1902 to 1924. What premier lightweight champ did he beat?
3. Name one of two welterweight champs Langford met in the ring.
4. Name the former middleweight champ who earned a draw with Langford.
5. Which light-heavyweight champ did Langford beat?
6. Why was Langford never crowned the champion in these divisions?
7. Langford gave Jack Johnson a stiff test before the latter became champion. What reason did Johnson offer for not giving Langford a title shot?
8. What boxer tangled with Langford in the longest series of bouts in boxing history?
9. Name two other boxers who fought Langford at least ten times.
10. Langford failed to finish only three bouts during his prime in a career that spanned 252 recorded bouts. Sam was stopped twice by Harry Wills and once by a "White Hope" contender. Name him.

46. HAMMERIN' HANK (15 pts.)

How well do you remember the buzz-saw fighter who rained non-stop punches onto overwhelmed opponents—Henry Armstrong?

1. *True or False*: Henry Armstrong is the only man in boxing history to hold three world titles simultaneously.
2. What three weight divisions did Armstrong reign over during his fifteen-year ring career?
3. How many times was "Hurricane Hank" put down for the ten-count in his 176 professional fights?
4. After losing three straight decisions to this rock-hard Mexican featherweight, Armstrong finally won a ten-round verdict over his once-unsolvable opponent on August 18, 1936. Who was his south-of-the-border ring nemesis?
5. Who did Henry knock out with a looping right to the jaw in the sixth round on October 29, 1937 to win the featherweight championship of the world?
6. Armstrong outgrew the featherweight division and sought the welterweight championship. Who did "Homicide Hank" easily decision over fifteen rounds to add a second title to his growing list of ring honors?

7. How many times did Armstrong successfully defend his welterweight title? (a) 5 (b) 8 (c) 11 (d) 14 (e) 20
8. Who was the first man to knock Armstrong down in a title contest?
9. New York booed Henry Armstrong when his split-decision victory over this lightweight champ was announced by master-of-ceremonies Harry Balogh. Who did Henry repeatedly foul enroute to his third world title?
10. How many times did Armstrong successfully defend his lightweight championship? (a) 0 (b) 3 (c) 7 (d) 10 (e) 14
11. To whom did Armstrong lose his lightweight title?
12. Who plucked the Human Buzz-Saw's third and only remaining crown from his head by winning a fifteen-round decision from Henry on October 4, 1940?
13. On March 1, 1940, Armstrong came close to adding a fourth world title to his ring accomplishments when he fought a draw with middleweight champion _____.
14. Which one of the following ring opponents did not defeat Armstrong? (a) Reuben Shank (b) Beau Jack (c) Ray Robinson (d) Baby Manuel (e) Barney Ross
15. What profession did Armstrong ironically turn to after hanging up his gloves?

47. THE TOY BUILLDOG (10 pts.)

Tangle with these questions on hard-punching Mickey Walker.

1. Walker fought for the welterweight title in his third year as a pro. Did he win?
2. Who did Walker defeat for the welterweight title?
3. *True or False*: Walker actively defended his welterweight title seven times.
4. Who took the welterweight title from him?
5. *True or False*: Walker won the middleweight title in his first attempt to step up to the heavier weight class.
6. Who did Walker beat to win the middleweight championship of the world?
7. How did Walker lose the middleweight title?
8. Did Walker ever vie for the light-heavy title?
9. Did Walker ever face any heavyweight competition in the ring?
10. Walker was stopped only twice in 148 recorded bouts. Who put the leash on the Toy Bulldog?

48. THE UNKNOWN TRIPLE-CHAMP (10 pts.)

Meet the challenge on one of boxing's super champs—Tony Canzoneri.

1. As an amateur champ, Canzoneri fought mainly in New York. Where was he born?
2. Tony fought for his first world title at the age of eighteen. Did he win?
3. Which title did he win first?
4. *True or False*: Canzoneri successfully defended his first world title eight times.
5. Name the other two boxing titles Canzoneri won during his illustrious career.
6. What distinction does Tony share with Henry Armstrong?
7. What was so unusual about Tony's loss of the lightweight title to Barney Ross?
8. Tony's twenty-one championship bouts rank sixth on the all-time list. What was

his win percentage for these title tilts? (a) 55% (b) 75% (c) 95% (d) 100%
9. *True or False*: Canzoneri won nineteen of his twenty-one title fights by a knockout.
10. How many times was Tony stopped in his fourteen-year ring career?

49. FISTIC FIRSTS (10 pts.)

See if you can remember these famous "firsts" in boxing history.

1. Who was the first black referee to handle a heavyweight championship bout?
2. Who was the first black woman judge?
3. Who was the first black to win a world title?
4. Who was the first black light-heavyweight champ?
5. Who was the first champ to regain his lost title?
6. Who was the first boxer to use a mouthpiece?
7. Who was the first champ to enter the movies?
8. Who were the first American-born boxers?
9. Who was the first heavyweight champ to box on foreign soil?
10. Who was the first modern heavyweight champion to change his mind about retirement and return to the ring?

50. RETURN OF THE CHAMPION (10 pts.)

All of these champs came out of retirement to box again. Can you identify which ones (1) re-won titles, (2) lost their title shots, and (3) were not offered another crack at the title?

1. Jim Corbett
2. James J. Jeffries
3. Joe Louis
4. Sugar Ray Robinson
5. Carl Bobo Olson
6. Henry Armstrong
7. Sammy Angott
8. Vincente Saldivar
9. Fidel LaBarba
10. Eder Jofre

51. WILL THE REAL WORLD CHAMPIONS PLEASE STAND UP? (11 pts.)

Identify the fighter in each weight division who did not rule as its champion during some point in his career.

1. *Heavyweight*: Marvin Hart, Ezzard Charles, Jimmy Ellis, Tom Sharkey, Primo Carnera
2. *Light-Heavyweight*: Mike McTigue, Maxie Rosenbloom, Billy Conn, Harold Johnson, Paul Berlenbach, Leo Lomski

3. *Middleweight*: George Chip, Paul Pender, Gorilla Jones, Cyclone Johnny Thompson, Ace Hudkins, Carl Olson, Terry Downes
4. *Junior-Middleweight*: Nino Benvenuti, Koichi Wajima, Denny Moyer, Sandro Mazzhingi, Stan Hayward, Freddie Little
5. *Welterweight*: Freddie Red Cochrane, Virgil Akins, Lou Brouillard, Ceferino Garcia, Honey Mellody, Curtis Cokes
6. *Junior-Welterweight*: Carlos Ortiz, Barney Ross, Tony Canzoneri, Frankie Klick, Eddie Perkins, Sandro Lopopolo, Battling Shaw
7. *Lightweight*: Lauro Salas, Ismael Laguna, Sammy Angott, Mando Ramos, Art Aragon, Al Singer, Rocky Kansas
8. *Junior-Lightweight*: Flash Elorde, Kid Chocolate, Hiroshi Kubayashi, Eddie Cannonball Martin, Tod Morgan, Johnny Dundee
9. *Featherweight*: Solly Smith, Young Griffo, Freddie Miller, Jose Legra, Davey Moore, Chalky Wright, Eugene Criqui
10. *Bantamweight*: Abe Goldstein, Charli Phil Rosenberg, Frankie Burns, Vic Toweel, Eder Jofre, Sixto Escobar
11. *Flyweight*: Pascual Perez, Jackie Brown, Chartai Chionoi, Rinty Monaghan, Fidel La Barba, Small Montana, Benny Lynch

52. OLYMPIC CHAMPIONS (15 pts.)

Try to answer these gold medal-winners about amateur Olympic boxing.

1. How many former Olympic gold medal-winners have gone on to win professional world titles?
2. In what weight class did Floyd Patterson win the gold medal at Helsinki in 1952?
3. *True or False*: Eighteen-year old Cassius Clay captured the heavyweight gold medal at the Rome Olympiad in 1960.
4. Name the dynamite-fisted Cuban who ripped apart America's Duane Bobick to win the Olympic gold medal for heavyweight boxing in 1972 at the tragedy-marred Munich Games.
5. After winning the Olympic gold medal in 1956 at Melbourne, this young heavyweight fought world champion Floyd Patterson for boxing's top prize in his very first professional bout. Who was this highly-touted puncher who was brought along a little bit too soon?
6. Who is the only man to win boxing gold medals at three consecutive Olympiads?
7. What heavyweight champion was once disqualified in the finals of Olympic Game competition?
8. How many rounds are there in an official Olympic boxing match?
9. Who is the only boxer to win gold medals for two different weight titles in the same Olympiad?
10. Who was the first Olympic champion to fight his way to the heavyweight championship of the world?
11. The Soviet Union first participated in Olympic boxing in: (a) 1904 (b) 1920 (c) 1932 (d) 1952 (e) 1956
12. When George Foreman won his gold medal at the 1968 Olympic Games, he waved a pair of tiny American flags in the center of the prize-ring. Where were the Olympics held the year of George's triumph?
13. *True or False*: Joe Frazier won the heavyweight gold medal in 1960 at the Rome Olympics.

14. What former Olympic flyweight gold medal-winner defeated Joe Dundee for the undisputed welterweight championship of the world in 1929?
15. Who was the only American boxer to win a gold medal at the 1972 Olympic Games at Munich?

53. PICK THE DECADE (10 pts.)

Pick the decade in which each of these champs were in their primes: 1880's, 1890's, 1900's, 1910's, 1920's, 1930's, 1940's, 1950's, 1960's, 1970's.

1. Ali, Griffith, Jofre.
2. Armstrong, Ross, Canzoneri, McLarnin, Kid Chocolate, Panama Al Brown.
3. Sullivan, "Nonpareil" Jack Dempsey, McAuliffe.
4. Louis, Conn, Zale, Ike Williams, Pep.
5. Jack Johnson, Dillon, Papke, Britton, Welsh, Ritchie, Herman, Wilde.
6. Corbett, Fitzsimmons, McCoy, Lavigne.
7. Marciano, Moore, Robinson, Gavilan, Saddler.
8. Frazier, Foster, Monzon, Napoles, Duran, Olivares.
9. O'Brien, Jeffries, Ryan, Ketchel, Walcott, Gans, McGovern.
10. Dempsey, Tunney, Loughran, Greb, Walker, Leonard, Villa, La Barba.

54. HOME TOWN BOYS I (15 pts.)

Can you match the fighter up with his real or adopted home town in which he fought a large number of his bouts?

1. Jim Jeffries
2. Harry Greb
3. Jersey Joe Walcott
4. Paul Pender
5. Ezzard Charles
6. Jack OBrien
7. Ingemar Johansson
8. Jack Dillon
9. Tony Zale
10. Rocky Marciano
11. Randy Turpin
12. Gene Fullmer
13. Freddie Cochrane
14. Curtis Cokes
15. Jose Napoles

a. Chicago
b. San Francisco
c. Boston
d. London
e. Philadelphia
f. Camden
g. Salt Lake City
h. Pittsburgh
i. Newark
j. Dallas
k. Mexico City
l. Gothenburg
m. Cincinnati
n. Indianapolis
o. Providence

55. HOME TOWN BOYS II (10 pts.)

Jab at a few more home-town match-ups.

1. Rocky Kansas
2. Joe Gans
3. Ismael Laguna
4. Carlos Teo Cruz
5. Battling Battalino
6. Pancho Villa
7. Johnny Famechon
8. Eddie Martin
9. Eder Jofre
10. Manuel Ortiz

a. Baltimore
b. Panama City
c. San Juan
d. Hartford
e. Melbourne
f. Buffalo
g. Brooklyn
h. Hollywood
i. Sao Paulo
j. Manila

QUESTIONS / 45

56. MAIN EVENTS: PHOTO QUIZ II (24 pts.)

1. How many times did light-heavyweight champ Bob Foster successfully defend his title before temporarily retiring in 1974?

2. Identify the fighter who twice won the welterweight title by defeating Young Corbett III and Barney Ross.

3. Name the two-time welterweight champion who decisioned Sugar Ray Robinson in 1957 to add the middleweight title to his ring laurels.

48 / *The World Championship Boxing Quizbook*

4. *True or False*: : Billy Papke won three middleweight titles by kayoing Stan Ketchel, Willie Lewis, and Marcel Moreau.

5. How many times did Ezzard Charles (pictured above) fight ring nemesis Jersey Joe Walcott for the heavyweight title?

6. Archie Moors (L) and Sugar Ray Robinson came within a "heat stroke" of meeting each other for the light-heavyweight title. What happened to prevent a dream match-up between these two great champs?

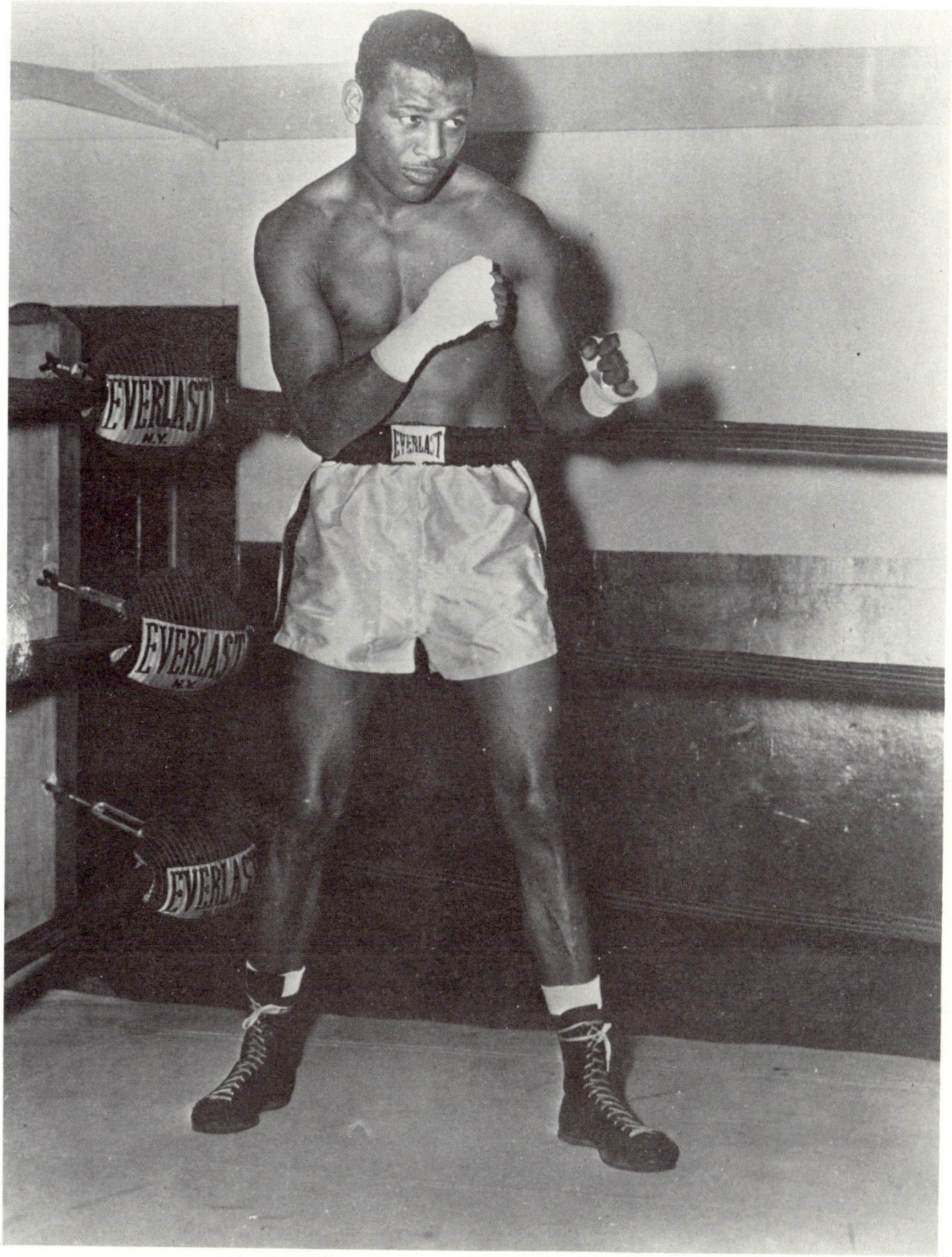
EVERLAST
N.Y.
EVERLAST
EVERLAST
N.Y.
EVERLAST

7. What was Floyd Patterson's "bread-and-butter" kayo punch?

QUESTIONS / 53

8. How many world titles did Barney Ross hold during his illustrious career?

54 / The World Championship Boxing Quizbook

9. Name the middleweight champ who once knocked heavyweight king Jack Johnson off his feet.

10. *True or False*: James J. Jeffries lost his coveted title to Jack Johnson on a fifteenth-round TKO on July 4, 1910.

56 / The World Championship Boxing Quizbook

11. How many fights has Muhammad Ali lost during his controversial career?

QUESTIONS / 57

12. What title did Kid McCoy win on March 2, 1896 by knocking out Tommy Ryan?

13. Aside from Jack Dempsey, how many other challengers did Gene Tunney engage in defense of his world heavyweight title?

QUESTIONS / 59

14. Who did *Ring* Editor Nat Fleischer pick as the "no. 1 heavyweight of all-time"?

15. Name the enterprising fight promoter who staged Dempsey's big-money bouts.

QUESTIONS / 61

16. Dick Tiger (L) and Gene Fullmer clashed three straight times for the middleweight title from 1962 to 1963. Who won each of these encounters?

17. *True or False:* Joe Louis was the underdog the night he kayoed Jimmy Braddock for the heavyweight title in 1937.

QUESTIONS / 63

18. Who did Harry Greb defeat for the middleweight title on August 31, 1923?

64 / The World Championship Boxing Quizbook

19. Rocky Marciano "fought" Muhammad Ali in a computerized "dream match" for the all-time heavyweight title. What was the outcome of this theatrically-staged ring battle?

20. *True or False*: Bob Fitzsimmons was the lightest man to hold the heavyweight title.

66 / The World Championship Boxing Quizbook

21. How old was Jack Dempsey when he won the heavyweight crown?

22. *True or False:* A middleweight by trade, Micky Walker lost two bids to win the heavyweight championship of the world.

68 / The World Championship Boxing Quizbook

23. What weight division did Willie Pep rule for almost eight years?

24. How many times did Henry Armstrong defend his first world crown—the featherweight title?

57. RING DEATHS (10 pts.)

Three boxers have died in world title matches and several others have been killed in non-title bouts. Can you recall these ring tragedies?

1. The welterweight who was killed challenging for the world title in 1947.
2. The welterweight who lost the title and his life in a 1962 bout.
3. The featherweight champ who was tragically killed in a 1963 title fight.
4. He died at the hands of a future heavyweight champ who seemed to "let up" on his opponents after this 1948 bout.
5. He succumbed to a future heavyweight champ in 1930.
6. He died in a fight with a future heavyweight champ on February 10, 1933.
7. He died of blood poisoning from an infected tooth which he injured in a 1925 bout.
8. He died from the effects of an eye operation in 1927.
9. What current heavyweight killed his opponent in a 1969 bout?
10. What 19th century title fight was won on a fatality?

58. BOXER VS. SLUGGER (10 pts.)

Does the bruising slugger usually get the better of the dancing boxer? Use your ring savvy to pick out the winner of each of these classic boxer-slugger confrontations.

ALTERNATE:

1. Corbett vs. Sullivan
2. Tunney vs. Dempsey
3. Conn vs. Louis
4. Braddock vs. Louis
5. Ali vs. Liston
6. Ali vs. Frazier
7. O'Brien vs. Ketchel
8. Greb vs. Walker
9. Ambers vs. Armstrong
10. Pep vs. Saddler

59. SPOT THE DIVISION (10 pts.)

Weigh-in and answer these questions about boxing's weight divisions.

1. Everyone knows the heavyweights are the power-division. But in what weight class are bouts among champs second only to the heavies in KO percentage?
2. What two "stepping-stone" divisions have the lowest KO percentages but usually produce top-notch challengers for the better-known heavier weight classes?
3. What is generally considered the most popular division after the heavyweights?
4. What division is closely identified with clever boxers?
5. Only six of the current eight divisions existed in 1900. What are the two newest major weight classes?

QUESTIONS / 71

6. Although early champions could alter the weight limits to their liking, one manager created a whole new division for his boxer. Which division was it?
7. Which two divisions have been most consistent in their weight limits?
8. The heavyweight division is the oldest weight class. Which division is the second oldest?
9. Which division leads all others in retiring its champions as undefeated titleholders?
10. One test of the overall balance and quality of a division is to determine the number of bouts that ended in draws. Which division has produced the most draws in bouts between champs?

60. THE HEAVYWEIGHTS (15 pts.)

Test your memory out on boxing's most-publicized weight divisions.

1. How many heavyweight champions regained their title after losing it in the ring?
2. Who was the only former heavyweight king to fight both Jack Dempsey and Joe Louis?
3. Who lost more fights than any other heavyweight champion of the world?
4. All but three heavyweight champs suffered a knockout during their ring career. Who are the members of this iron-jawed trio?
5. After retiring as undefeated heavyweight champion of the world, Jim Jeffries announced that a fight would be staged between Marvin Hart and the light-heavyweight champion to determine his successor. Who did Hart knock out in the twelfth round at Reno, Nevada on July 3, 1905 to win boxing's most coveted prize?
6. Rearrange these former champs into the chronological order in which they held the heavyweight title: Tunney, Schmeling, Carnera, Baer, Sharkey, Braddock, and Louis.
7. What former heavyweight champ went on to capture the light-heavyweight title more than five years after losing the heavyweight crown?
8. Name the free-swinging Argentinian who sent Jack Dempsey crashing out of the ring onto a newsman's typewriter during the first round of his unsuccessful bid to capture the heavyweight championship of the world.
9. This 37-year old ring veteran became the oldest man to ascend the heavyweight throne by knocking out Ezzard Charles in the seventh round of a 1951 title bout. Who is he?
10. How many times has the heavyweight championship changed hands via a decision?
11. Which heavyweight champ recorded the most career knockouts?
12. Which champ had the best KO percentage of all bouts fought?
13. Which heavyweight king had the best career win percentage?
14. Which champ fought the most times?
15. Who held the heavyweight title for the longest period of time?

61. THE LIGHT-HEAVIES (10 pts.)

Conquer these heavyweight onlookers.

1. What is the light-heavy weight limit?
2. Who was the division's first champion?
3. Which champ fought the most total career bouts?
4. Which champ had the highest career win percentage?
5. Which champ had the highest career KO percentage?
6. Which champ held the title the longest?
7. Which champ made the most title defenses?
8. Did any champ ever regain the title?
9. Many light-heavy champs moved up to vie for the heavyweight championship. How many made it?
10. Name five of the eight light-heavy champs who fought for the heavyweight title.

62. THE MIDDLEWEIGHTS (10 pts.)

1. What is the middleweight pound limit?
2. What early middleweight's name was later adopted by a prominent heavyweight?
3. Which middleweight champ recorded the highest career win percentage?
4. Which middleweight champ has the highest career KO percentage?
5. Which champ held the title the longest?
6. Which champ made the most title defenses?
7. Which champ engaged in the most total bouts during his career?
8. Did any champ ever regain the title?
9. Did any middleweight champ move up to win the light-heavy title?
10. Did any middleweight ever compete in a heavyweight title bout?

63. THE WELTERWEIGHTS (10 pts.)

1. What is the welterweight pound limit?
2. What early welterweight champ gave his name to a later heavyweight titleholder?
3. Which champ had the highest career win percentage?
4. Which champ racked up the highest career KO percentage?
5. Which champ held the title the longest?
6. Which champ made the most title defenses?
7. Which welter champ led his division in total career bouts?
8. Which two champs made a career of fighting each other, meeting in some twenty bouts?
9. Name the two famous welterweight non-champs who shared the same last name.
10. Name three of the five welterweights who successfully moved up to become middleweight champion.

64. THE LIGHTWEIGHTS (10 pts.)

1. What is the lightweight pound limit?

2. Between 1885 and 1925 there were nine notable lightweight champs. Name five of these titleholders.
3. A tough one! Between 1930 and 1940 Tony Canzoneri (two times), Barney Ross, Lou Ambers (two times), and Henry Armstrong were mixing it up in a topsy-turvy lightweight title scramble. Can you reconstruct the chain of events during this period?
4. Which champ has the best career win percentage?
5. Which champ has the best career KO percentage?
6. Which champ held the title the longest?
7. Which champ had the most title defenses?
8. Which champ fought the most total bouts during his career?
9. What champ held some version of the title from 1945 to 1951?
10. Five lightweights regained the title—Canzoneri, Ambers, Bob Montgomery, James Carter, and Carlos Ortiz. Which one held the title three times?

65. THE FEATHERWEIGHTS (10 pts.)

1. What is the featherweight pound limit?
2. Name the quadroon boxing out of Boston who became the first important featherweight back in the 1890s.
3. What "bulldog" featherweight won the title in 1900 and instantly earned the reputation for being one of the greatest featherweights of all time?
4. Which champ had the best career win percentage?
5. Which champ racked up the best career KO percentage?
6. Which champ held the title the longest?
7. Which champ had the most title defenses?
8. Which champ fought the most total bouts during his career?
9. What Cuban boxer, who learned to fight by studying films of the great lightweight Joe Gans, was a popular New York state featherweight champ?
10. Name three of the five featherweights who regained their title.

66. THE BANTAMWEIGHTS (10 pts.)

1. What is the bantamweight pound limit?
2. Which two early champs moved up to become featherweight titleholders?
3. Name two of the four highly-regarded bantamweight champs who dominated the division between 1910 and 1925.
4. Which champ had the highest career win percentage?
5. Which champ recorded the highest career KO percentage?
6. Which champ held the title the longest?
7. Which champ made the most title defenses?
8. Which champ fought the most total bouts during his career?
9. Name two of the four champs who regained the title.
10. Who was the tallest bantam champ?

67. THE FLYWEIGHTS (10 pts.)

1. What is the flyweight pound limit?

2. Who became the first flyweight champ in 1916 when the weight limit was set at 108 pounds?
3. Name two of the four legendary champs who followed the first flyweight titleholder.
4. Between 1932 and 1950, England, Ireland, and Scotland passed the title around among six champs. Name two of them.
5. Which champ had the highest career win percentage?
6. Which champ had the highest career KO percentage?
7. Which champ held the title the longest?
8. Which champ made the most title defenses?
9. Which champ fought the most total bouts during his career?
10. How many flyweight champs regained their title?

68. THE JUNIOR WEIGHT TITLES (10 pts.)

1. What are the two most popular junior weight divisions?
2. Name one of the two junior-welter titleholders who was also a well-known lightweight champ.
3. Name one of the three junior-lightweight champs who also held the featherweight title.
4. Which junior division did the W.B.A. create in 1962?
5. Who is the only champ to rise above this recently-created division to the championship of a heavier weight class?
6. Have the junior weight divisions ever been used as stepping stones to higher titles?
7. What three junior divisions were established in New York before 1920 but didn't catch on?
8. What two junior titles have appeared mainly as promotions during the past few years?
9. Which Argentinian junior-welter compiled a fantastic 97% career win percentage?
10. Which flashy junior-lightweight champ held the title for over seven years but failed in two attempts at the lightweight title and in one shot at the featherweight title?

69. THE ALL-TIME GREATS (15 pts.)

Can you keep pace with these premier fighters from all of boxing's weight divisions?

1. Which champ has the best career KO percentage?
2. Which champ compiled the best career win percentage?
3. Which champ held the title the longest?
4. Which champ made the most title defenses?
5. Which champ appeared in the most title bouts?
6. Which champ fought the most total career bouts?
7. Which champ racked up the longest win streak?
8. Which champ scored the most total knockouts?
9. What bout was chosen by a nationwide poll of sportswriters and broadcasters as the biggest boxing story of the past 75 years?
10. Which boxer is the all-time leading money-earner?

11. Which champ holds the record for most career wins by decision?
12. Which champ piled up the most consecutive knockouts in title bouts?
13. Which two champs engaged in title bouts during three different decades?
14. Several champs were never stopped. Which one had the most total career bouts without being KO'd or TKO'd?
15. Which heavyweight champ fought the most career bouts without being stopped?

70. BATTLES OF THE CENTURY (10 pts.)

Peek in and see if you can remember these celebrated bouts from boxing's glorious past.

1. First bare-knuckle match staged between a black and white fighter.
2. Winner of rematch of previous bout.
3. He held John L. Sullivan to a 39-round draw in 1888.
4. Much-ballyhooed match between undefeated black and white combatants, July 4, 1910.
5. International contest between an American heavyweight and an outclassed Frenchman.
6. Exciting brawl between an American heavyweight and a wild-swinging Argentinian.
7. Classic rematch between an American heavyweight and a German.
8. Date and location of first Ali-Frazier bout.
9. Date and location of second Ali-Frazier bout.
10. Date and location of third Ali-Frazier bout.

71. THE CORNERMEN I (10 pts.)

Match the boxing champion with his crafty and resourceful trainer or manager.

1. Jack Dempsey   (a) Gil Clancy
2. Emile Griffith   (b) George Little
3. Muhammad Ali   (c) Johnny Ray
4. Jack Johnson   (d) Lou Viscusi
5. Carmen Basilio   (e) Angelo Dundee
6. George Foreman   (f) Jack "Doc" Kearns
7. Billy Conn   (g) Willie Ketchum
8. Lew Jenkins   (h) Johnny DeJohn
9. Floyd Patterson   (i) Dick Sadler
10. Willie Pep   (j) Cus D'Amato

72. THE CORNERMEN II (10 pts.)

Can you "patch up" these fighters with their cut-wise handlers?

1. Rocky Marciano   (a) Jesse Goss
2. Sugar Ray Robinson   (b) William A. Brady

3. Henry Armstrong
4. Max Schmeling
5. Rocky Graziano
6. Ike Williams
7. Max Baer
8. James J. Corbett
9. Joe Frazier
10. Joe Louis

(c) Al Weill
(d) Irving Cohen
(e) Yank Durham
(f) Joe Jacobs
(g) Jack Blackburn
(h) Ancil Hoffman
(i) George Gainford
(j) Eddie Mead

73. BIG-TIME OPERATORS (10 pts.)

Match these famous fight managers and promoters with their favorite boxing attractions.

1. Joe Gould
2. Harry Mendel
3. Jack Kearns
4. Pete Reilly
5. Mike Jacobs
6. Joe Jacobs
7. Jimmy Johnston
8. Billy McCarney
9. Dan Morgan
10. Eddie Mead

(a) Max Schmeling, Tony Galento
(b) Joe Louis, Billy Conn
(c) Jack Dempsey, Mickey Walker
(d) Bob Pastor, Abe Simon
(e) Joe Lynch, Henry Armstrong
(f) Tony Galento
(g) Jack Britton, Battling Levinsky
(h) Max Schmeling
(i) Andre Routis, Petey Scalzo
(j) Jim Braddock

74. OUTSIDE NOTABLES (10 pts.)

Can you match these famous non-boxing personages with the nature of their brief involvement with pugilism.

1. Adolf Hitler
2. Wyatt Earp
3. Judge Roy Bean
4. Bat Masterson
5. Jack London
6. Judge Kenesaw Mountain Landis
7. Arthur Conan Doyle
8. George Bernard Shaw
9. Ernest Hemingway
10. Norman Mailer

(a) Boxing writer for *Morning Telegraph*
(b) Proposed referee for Dempsey-Carpentier bout
(c) Referee in Fitzsimmons-Sharkey fix
(d) Enforced Mann Act on Jack Johnson
(e) Tunney confidant
(f) Wrote short story on Stanley Ketchel
(g) Entertained Schmeling
(h) Wrote about heavyweights' egos
(i) Handled arrangements for Fitzsimmons-Maher bout
(j) Boxing writer during "White Hope" Era

75. THE BARONS OF BOXING (10 pts.)

Can you identify these boxing associations of the past and present from their initials?

1. W.B.A.
2. W.B.C.
3. E.B.U.
4. N.B.A.
5. I.b.
6. C.C.C.
7. J.B.C.
8. N.Y.S.A.C.
9. N.A.B.F.
10. B.B.B.C.

76. UNSUNG GIANT-KILLERS (10 pts.)

Fill in the blanks with the only fighter to have knocked out these ring immortals.

1. Seeking to become only the fifth triple champion in boxing history, Sugar Ray Robinson collapsed from the sweltering 104 degree heat in an unsuccessful bid to wrest the light-heavyweight title from _____ on June 25, 1952 at New York's Yankee Stadium.
2. Two years prior to ascending the throne of light-heavyweight king, Jose Torres was counted out in the fifth round of his stormy contest with left-hooking Latin blockbuster _____ on May 26, 1963 in San Juan, Puerto Rico.
3. Five years after losing his title to Britisher Freddie Welsch, Willie Ritchie was kayoed in the eighth round by the great lightweight king _____ on April 28, 1919 at Newark, New Jersey.
4. Power-punching featherweight champion Sandy Saddler was stopped by _____ in his professional fight on March 21, 1944 at Hartford, Connecticut.
5. Several years before capturing the welterweight title in 1929, Jackie Fields was taken out in two rounds by the "Baby Face" Kid who likewise became welterweight champ, _____.
6. Hard-hitting junior-welterweight and lightweight champ Carlos Ortiz was halted in his final bout on September 20, 1972 by former lightwight titleholder, Scotland's _____.
7. Tough middleweight champion Johnny Wilson was kayoed in the third round of his meeting with future titleholder _____ on December 9, 1924 at New York.
8. Legendary great Jack Dempsey was battered to the canvas four times in suffering a knockout defeat in his 1917 clash with the experienced _____ in Murray, Utah.
9. Former heavyweight king Tommy Burns was starched in seven heats in his final professional bout by future British champion _____ on July 16, 1920.
10. Bantamweight champ Pete Herman TKO'd in thirteen rounds several years before winning the title by _____, who waged three unsuccessful attempts to capture the championship against Johnny Coulon, Kid Williams, and, years later, Herman himself.

77. BOWING OUT (10 pts.)

Match the boxing champion with his last ring opponent.

1. James J. Corbett
2. Jim Jeffries
3. Jack Sharkey
4. Max Baer
5. Joe Louis
6. Jersey Joe Walcott
7. Floyd Patterson
8. Barney Ross
9. Jimmy McLarnin
10. John Henry Lewis

(a) Lou Nova
(b) Muhammad Ali
(c) Jack Johnson
(e) Lou Ambers
(f) Jim Jeffries
(g) Henry Armstrong
(h) Joe Louis

78. THE FINAL COUNT (10 pts.)

Identify the fighting champion who died as a result of the following injuries, accidents, or illnesses.

1. Drug overdose, 1970
2. Plane crash, 1969
3. Shot in brawl in New York's Hell's Kitchen, 1925
4. Lateral sclerosis, 1975
5. Died on operating table of hemmorage while having plastic surgery performed on his punched-in nose, 1926
6. Double pneumonia, 1917
7. Heart attack while refereeing the Bobby Williams—Mario Roman six-rounder at St. Nick's Arena, New York, 1947
8. Smashed his Lincoln roadster into power pole, 1946
9. Infected teeth after failing to have them extracted, 1925
10. Shot in back by jealous farm hand, 1910

79. THEIR POST-GLORY YEARS I (10 pts.)

Match these champs with their prominent occupations or achievements after retiring from the ring.

1. County sheriff
2. Mink rancher
3. Sports editor of the *Police Gazette*
4. Prison recreation director
5. Boxing coach for Hollywood movie actors
6. Caesar's Palace Hotel host
7. Flycasting exhibitioner
8. TV celebrity and commercial pitchman
9. Fountainbleau Hotel bootblack
10. Stage actor

(a) Beau Jack
(b) Mushy Callahan
(c) Rocky Graziano
(d) Max Schmeling
(e) James J. Corbett
(f) Jersey Joe Walcott
(g) Paul Pender
(h) Jack Sharkey
(i) Mickey Walker
(j) Joe Louis

80. THEIR POST-GLORY YEARS II (10 pts.)

Try to redeem yourself in this "re-match" of boxing champions with their line of work after exiting the ring.

1. Broadway restauranteur
2. Co-star in movie *Huckleberry Finn*
3. New Orleans cafe owner
4. Hollywood actor and youth foundation organizer
5. Temperance reformer
6. Sugar broker on Wall Street commodities market
7. Fight trainer
8. Columnist, author, and associate editor of *Boxing Illustrated*
9. Portrayed Ethiopian General in opera *Aida*
10. Manager of tassle dancer Sally Keith

(a) Pete Herman
(b) Archie Moore
(c) Tommy Loughran
(d) Jose Torres
(e) John L. Sullivan
(f) Johnny Wilson
(g) Sugar Ray Robinson
(h) Sandy Saddler
(i) Jack Dempsey
(j) Jack Johnson

81. TRADEMARKS (15 pts.)

Match the boxer with his easily-recognizable trademark.

1. Handle-bar moustache
2. Meatless crash-diets
3. Scowl
4. Plastered-down hair parted in middle
5. Star of David on boxing trunks and clowning tactics
6. Expressionless face
7. Temper tantrums
8. Bowing to crowd when introduced by ring announcer
9. Hitching up emerald-green trunks with forearms
10. Reading Shakespeare, Shaw, and scientific textbooks
11. Pompadour hair style
12. Wearing false beard and glasses to disguise himself after losses
13. Green satin robe with Shamrock stitched on back
14. Hovering over downed opponent to hit him before he had a chance to rise
15. "Golden smile" and taunting opponents

(a) Harry Greb
(b) Jack Johnson
(c) Benny Leonard
(d) Jack Sharkey
(e) Joe Louis
(f) James J. Corbett
(g) Gene Tunney
(h) Archie Moore
(i) Floyd Patterson
(j) Joe Frazier
(k) Tony Galento
(l) Sonny Liston
(m) Max Baer
(n) John L. Sullivan
(o) Jack Dempsey

82. YOU'RE THE JUDGE (10 pts.)

How did each of these historic fights end?

1. *Jess Willard vs. Frank Moran, March 25, 1916:*
   (a) Willard KO 6 (b) Willard TKO 9 (c) Willard TKO 11 (d) Moran KO 8 (e) No decision
2. *Joe Frazier vs. Terry Daniels, January 15, 1972:*
   (a) Frazier KO 1 (b) Frazier KO 9 (c) Frazier KO 12 (d) Frazier TKO 4 (e) Daniels KO 9
3. *Ingemar Johansson vs. Eddie Machen, September 14, 1958:*
   (a) Johansson KO 11 (b) Johansson KO 9 (c) Johansson decision 12 (d) Machen KO 7 (e) Machen decision 12
4. *Eder Jofre vs. Eloy Sanchez, November 18, 1960:*
   (a) Jofre KO 6 (b) Jofre TKO 11 (c) Sanchez KO 7 (d) Sanchez TKO 11 (e) Sanchez decision 15
5. *Young Corbett vs. Terry McGovern, November 28, 1901:*
   (a) Corbett KO 2 (b) Corbett TKO 8 (c) Corbett TKO 12 (d) McGovern KO 8 (e) McGovern TKO 11
6. *Freddie Mills vs. Gus Lesnevich, July 26, 1948:*
   (a) Mills KO 6 (b) Mills TKO 10 (c) Mills decision 15 (d) Lesnevich KO 8 (e) Lesnevich TKO 13
7. *Mike Quarry vs. Bob Foster, June 27, 1972:*
   (a) Quarry TKO 10 (b) Quarry decision 15 (c) Foster KO 4 (d) Foster TKO 12 (e) Foster decision 15
8. *Carmen Basilio vs. Kid Gavilan, September 18, 1953:*
   (a) Basilio KO 6 (b) Basilio TKO 9 (c) Basilio decision 15 (d) Gavilan TKO 11 (c) Gavilan decision 15
9. *Dick Tiger vs. Jose Torres, December 16, 1966 and Mary 16, 1967:*
   (a) Tiger KO 11 (b) Tiger decision 15 (c) Torres KO 13 (d) Torres TKO 7 (e) Torres decision 15
10. *Billy Petrolle vs. Tony Canzoneri, November 4, 1932:*
    (a) Petrolle KO 8 (b) Petrolle TKO 9 (c) Petrolle decision 15 (d) Canzoneri TKO 6 (e) Canzoneri decision 15

83. DIRTY FIGHTERS (10 pts.)

Some boxers will try to win any way they can. Protect yourself from low blows by naming these "streetfighters."

1. The power-punching welterweight who once lost five rounds on fouls in a title bout.
2. A welterweight noted for being dirty yet never lost a bout on a foul. He took the title from Armstrong.
3. Middleweight champ who thumbed a lot (and heeled, gouged, butted, etc.)
4. Stocky heavyweight champ who hit you wherever he could with his short arms.
5. Tall heavyweight who grabbed, held, and often toppled to the floor with his opponents.
6. Middleweight with reputation for butting who gave Ketchel trouble.

7. A journeyman light-heavy non-champ from Georgia who held and wrestled.
8. Lightweight who lost the title on a foul to Willie Ritchie and his bid to regain the crown on a foul to Freddy Welsh.
9. A middleweight brawler from New York City.
10. A notorious welterweight fouler who bit Joe Walcott in a title bout.

84. REMEMBER WHEN . . .? (10 pts.)

Rearrange these memorable bouts in chronological order.

1. "Bad boy" Rocky Graziano stages miraculous rally in blood-splattered sixth round to stop middleweight champion Tony Zale and capture world title.
2. Eye-gouging master Harry Greb outpoints Johnny Wilson over fifteen rounds to become middleweight champion of the world.
3. Ferocious-hitting Stanley Ketchel knocks out bitter rival Billy Papke in the eleventh round to regain middleweight championship he had lost via kayo to Papke two and one-half months earlier.
4. Briton Randy Turpin pulls off stunning upset by dethroning middleweight champ Ray Robinson on fifteen-round points decision, thus handing the Sugar Man only his second loss in twelve years.
5. Miami Beach southpaw Willie Pastrano decisions tough Harold Johnson to win light-heavyweight title.
6. Lightweight champion Benny Leonard survives a vicious left to the chin in the eighth round by momentarily distracting challenger Lew Tendler's attention and wins newspaper verdict in twelve-round no-decision bout.
7. Out-of-shape featherweight champ George Dixon survives seven knockdowns during eighth round but fails to answer bell for ninth against younger opponent Terry McGovern.
8. Dynamite-fisted Sandy Saddler scores fourth-round knockout of champion Willie Pep in their first of four ring meetings to win featherweight championship of the world.
9. Frenchman Georges Carpentier kayos former welterweight champ Ted Kid Lewis in only successful defense of his light-heavyweight title when the latter drops his guard to turn to referee Joe Palmer to protest his innocence of ring infraction.
10. Battling Nelson knocks out Baltimore Negro Joe Gans in the seventeenth round to claim world lightweight title.

85. WIN, LOSE, . . . OR DRAW (10 pts.)

How many of boxing's classic draw bouts do you remember?

1. How many heavyweight title fights have ended in a draw?
2. Name the legendary "Black Prince" of boxing who fought James J. Corbett to a gruelling 61-round draw on May 21, 1891 in San Francisco.
3. Which one of the following tilts did not end in a draw?
   (a) Patterson vs. Quarry I, June 9, 1967, ten rounds
   (b) Sharkey vs. Heeney, January 13, 1928, 12 rounds
   (c) Schmeling vs. Uzcudun, May 13, 1934, 12 rounds
   (d) Gavilan vs. Basilio, September 18, 1953, 15 rounds

4. What was the name of the iron-fisted, 160-pound Jewish fighter who held heavyweight champs Bob Fitzsimmons and James J. Jeffries to draws?
5. After winning the title by knocking out Johnny Coulon in three rounds, this bantamweight champion twice defended his title with bitterly-contested draws against Frankie Burns and Pete Herman. Name this titleholder who eventually lost his crown on a twenty-round points decision to Herman on January 9, 1917 in New Orleans.
6. Name the British 160-pound ring tactician who slashed through the mud enroute to a thirty-nine-round draw with the great John L. Sullivan in a world championship title match fought under bare-knuckle rules at Chantilly, France on March 10, 1888.
7. What undefeated lightweight champion was floored three times by Jem Carney and rescued from defeat by a gathering of ringside friends in a 74-round draw fought during early morning hours in a Massachusetts barn on November 16, 1887?
8. After losing the welterweight title he held from December 18, 1901 to April 30, 1904, this "Barbados Demon" fought a twenty-round draw two weeks later with his conqueror Dixie Kid in an unsuccessful bid to recapture the crown. Who was this black, skin-headed namesake of a future heavyweight champion of the world?
9. Match the boxers who once fought to a draw decision in a championship bout:
    (1) Abe Attell   (a) Mysterious Billy Smith
    (2) Frank Erne   (b) Owen Moran
    (3) Tommy Ryan   (c) Jack Daly
    (4) George Kid Lavigne   (d) Philadelphia Jack O'Brien
    (5) George Dixon   (e) Young Griffo
10. Relinquishing his claim to the middleweight title to fight in the heavyweight division, he battled top contender Jack Sharkey to a disputed fifteen-round draw on July 22, 1931, only eleven months before the latter won the world heavyweight championship. Who was this bruising former middleweight *and* welterweight champ with the devastating body attack?

86. FIX! (10 pts.)

If you know the cirumstances surrounding each of these alleged fixes, you'll know whether the ending was pre-arranged or on-the-level.

1. Tom Sharkey WF 9 over Jim Corbett
2. Tom Sharkey WF 8 over Bob Fitzsimmons
3. Terry McGovern KO 2 over Joe Gans
4. Billy Fox TKO 4 over Jake LaMotta
5. Ali KO 11 over Liston
6. Jess Willard KO 26 over Jack Johnson
7. Marvin Hart W 20 over Jack Johnson
8. Jack Britton WF 13 over Benny Leonard
9. Nonpareil Jack Dempsey WF 32 over George LaBlanche
10. Ad Wolgast KO 13 over Joe Rivers

87. MEMORABLE QUOTES (10 pts.)

See if you can identify these familiar voices from Boxing Past.

1. "Jeffries must emerge from his alfalfa farm and remove the smile from Johnson's face. It's up to you, Jeff!"
2. "We wuz robbed!"
3. "Last one up's a sissy!"
4. "I can lick any man in the house!"
5. "I think it's time for me to quit when I get whupped by a 46-year-old man and a computer that was made in Alabama."
6. "I waited two years for the revenge and now I got it."
7. "... I would have moidered da bum!"
8. "I think the only way I could have beaten Joe was with a baseball bat."
9. "This is a tough deal to be counted out over a sneaking little punch..."
10. "He can run, but he can't hide."

88. PUGILISTIC STYLES (10 pts.)

Match the champion with the punch or boxing style which best characterized his ring performance.

1. Kid McCoy
2. Ingemar Johansson
3. Frank Moran
4. Kid Gavilan
5. Floyd Patterson
6. James J. Jeffries
7. Muhammad Ali
8. Bob Fitzsimmons
9. Rocky Marciano
10. Harry Greb

(a) Solar plexus
(b) Bolo
(c) Shuffle
(d) Corkscrew
(e) Peek-a-boo
(f) Mary Ann
(g) Thumbing
(h) Suzie Q
(i) Crouch
(j) Toonder

89. PICK THE ROUND (10 pts.)

How many rounds did each of the following bouts last?

1. "White Hope" Jess Willard KO's black champion Jack Johnson with right cross to capture heavyweight title, Havana, Cuba, April 5, 1915.
2. Floyd Patterson becomes first man in boxing history to regain heavyweight crown by flattening Ingemar Johansson with vicious left hook, Polo Grounds, New York, June 21, 1960.
3. Former heavyweight champ Max Schmeling pummels unbeaten Joe Louis with barrage of overhand rights en route to stunning upset knockout victory, Yankee Stadium, New York, June 19, 1936.
4. Challenger James J. Jeffries uses his 38-pound weight advantage to flatten 37-year old champion Bob Fitzsimmons, Coney Island, New York, June 9, 1899.

84 / *The World Championship Boxing Quizbook*

5. Underdog challenger Jack Dempsey destroys behemoth champ Jess Willard with savage two-fisted attack in scorching 102 degree heat, Maumee Bay, Toledo, Ohio, July 4, 1919.
6. Boxing's "black sheep" Rocky Graziano survives early knockdown to render middleweight champ Tony Zale helpless on ropes in title-winning TKO victory, Chicago Stadium, Illinois, July 16, 1947.
7. Trailing on points on all official scorecards, champion Joe Louis catches over-anxious challenger Billy Conn with thundering right hand KO blow to retain heavyweight crown, Polo Grounds, New York, June 18, 1941.
8. "Gentleman Jim" Corbett astounds the boxing world by dancing circles around, then knocking out seemingly-invincible heavyweight champion John L. Sullivan in classic-boxer-slugger confrontation, Olympic Club of New Orleans, Louisiana, September 7, 1892.
9. Unbeaten challenger Rocky Marciano picks himself off canvas in first round to topple champion Jersey Joe Walcott with crushing right-hand knockout punch after trailing on points, Philadelphia, Pennsylvania, September 23, 1952.
10. Heavily-favored champion Sonny Liston quits on stool with injured shoulder as brash challenger Cassius Clay becomes new heavyweight king, Miami Beach, Florida, February 25, 1964.

90. CLASSIC FIGHT SERIES (10 pts.)

Name the opponents in these famous fight series.

1. Two black heavyweights who met 23 times
2. Two welterweight champs who met 20 times
3. Two light-heavyweights who met 10 times
4. A heavyweight champ and a middleweight champ who met five times
5. Two flyweights, one a champ, who met 10 times
6. Two champs, a lightweight and a featherweight, who met 8 times
7. Opponent of Jack Johnson in 10 bouts
8. Ring foe of Archie Moore in five contests
9. Middleweight champ who was defeated four times by Sugar Ray Robinson
10. Nemesis of Henry Armstrong who split six decisions with "Homicide Hank"

91. CHAMPIONSHIP REIGNS (16 pts.—2 pts. each)

Place each series of champions into the chronological order in which they reigned as king of their respective weight division (applies to first reign as champion).

1. *Flyweight*: Benny Lynch, Pascual Perez, Jackie Brown, Frankie Genaro, Fidel La Barba, Pone Kingpetch, Midget Wolgast, Pancho Villa, Chartchai Chionoi, Jimmy Wilde.
2. *Bantamweight*: Joe Lynch, George Dixon, Manuel Ortiz, Panama Al Brown, Pete Herman, Charlie Phil Rosenberg, Eder Jofre, Lionel Rose, Johnny Coulon, Sixto Escobar.
3. *Featherweight*: Johnny Kilbane, Henry Armstrong, Terry McGovern, George Dixon, Vincente Saldivar, Abe Attell, Petey Sarron, Willie Pep, Jose Legra, Battling Battalino.

4. *Lightweight*: Joe Brown, Lou Ambers, Joe Gans, Carlos Ortiz, George Kid Lavigne, Battling Nelson, Ike Williams, Tony Canzoneri, Willie Ritchie, Sammy Mandell.
5. *Welterweight*: Kid Gavilan, Ted Kid Lewis, Sugar Ray Robinson, Jimmy McLarnin, Pete Latzo, Carmen Basilio, Emile Griffith, Henry Armstrong, Mysterious Billy Smith, Barney Ross.
6. *Middleweight*: Marcel Thil, Al McCoy, Harry Greb, Stanley Ketchel, Tony Zale, Nino Benvenuti, Johnny Wilson, Mickey Walker, Jake LaMotta, Tiger Flowers.
7. *Light-Heavyweight*: Archie Moore, Tommy Loughran, Maxie Rosenbloom, Jose Torres, Billy Conn, Gus Lesnevich, Georges Carpentier, Joey Maxim, John Henry Lewis, Jack Dillon.
8. *Heavyweight*: James J. Jeffries, Jack Johnson, Jack Dempsey, Primo Carnera, Jess Willard, Joe Louis, Ezzard Charles, Jersey Joe Walcott, Marvin Hart, Rocky Marciano.

92. INTERNATIONAL FLAVOR I (15 pts.)

Match these boxing notables with their native countries.

1. Joe Walcott (welterweight)		(a)	Nigeria
2. Eder Jofre		(b)	Panama
3. Jimmy McLarnin		(c)	Philippines
4. Arturo Godoy		(d)	Virgin Islands
5. Antonio Cervantes		(e)	Scotland
6. Tom Bogs		(f)	Denmark
7. Carlos Teo Cruz		(g)	Dominican Republic
8. Laszlo Papp		(h)	Hungary
9. Bunny Sterling		(i)	Jamaica
10. Tom Heeney		(j)	New Zealand
11. Dick Tiger		(k)	Barbados
12. Peppermint Frazier		(l)	Brazil
13. Ceferino Garcia		(m)	Canada
14. Peter Jackson		(n)	Chile
15. Ken Buchanan		(o)	Colombia

93. INTERNATIONAL FLAVOR II (10 pts.)

Take another shot at matching up boxers with their homelands.

1. Battling Siki		(a)	Venezuela
2. Jose Legra		(b)	Wales
3. Fritz Chervet		(c)	Yugoslavia
4. Matt Donovan		(d)	Mexico
5. Young Perez		(e)	Puerto Rico
6. Alfredo Marcano		(f)	Senegal
7. Tommy Farr		(g)	Spain
8. Yuan Preberg		(h)	Switzerland
9. Lauro Salas		(i)	Trinidad
10. Sixto Escobar		(j)	Tunisia

94. BOXING TIDBITS I (15 pts.)

1. Who were the only two champs who died while holding the title?
2. Who was the oldest boxer to engage in a title bout?
3. What was unusual about the Carruthers-Songkitrat bantamweight title bout?
4. What was unusual about junior-lightweight Hiroshi Kobayashi's six title defenses?
5. Who was the shortest of all champs?
6. What manager was associated with titlists in three different divisions at the same time?
7. What journeyman middleweight met ten world champs and seven other contenders who fought for a crown?
8. Who was unlucky enough to fight an Irishman on St. Patrick's Day in Dublin, Ireland?
9. Who was the smallest heavyweight to fight in a title match?
10. Who were the two smallest contenders to engage in a heavyweight match?
11. What two fighters combined for the "heaviest" heavyweight match?
12. Who was the favorite in each of the three Ali-Frazier bouts?
13. What black boxer received $50,000 for signing up for a match he never fought with Jack Dempsey?
14. Who was chosen in 1972 by the magazine *World Sports* as the top international sportsman of the decade?
15. How did Young Stribling die?

95. BOXING TIDBITS II (10 pts.)

Take out your mouthpiece and chomp down on these boxing tidbits.

1. Two middleweight champs' deaths were connected with eye operations. Who were they?
2. What fighter had lost 47 times when he challenged Sandy Saddler for the featherweight title?
3. What bantamweight champ did not turn pro until he was thirty years old?
4. Who was the only man to referee a heavyweight title fight before boxing in one?
5. Who was the only champ to win and lose a title in one-round bouts?
6. Who was stopped only once before, but twelve times after seeing his opponent die in the ring?
7. Which two heavyweight champs refereed championship bouts in their division?
8. What boxer lost three titles in one bout?
9. Who lost a title while winning a title defense of that title?
10. Harry Greb won and lost the middleweight title from southpaws. Name them.

96. BOXING TIDBITS III (10 pts.)

Identify each of these famous boxing celebrities.

1. Editor of *Ring*
2. Jeffries' last opponent before retiring as undefeated world heavyweight champion in 1904
3. His New York restaurant was recently closed
4. Bantamweight champ known for "whirlwind" style
5. Former long-time ring announcer at Madison Square Garden
6. Welsh featherweight champ nicknamed "Peerless"
7. Boxing historian who purchased Jack Johnson's "confession" that he had thrown the Willard fight
8. Only man to hold three simultaneous world titles
9. Nickname of heavyweight king Jack Dempsey's namesake
10. First light-heavyweight champion

97. PICK YOUR OWN TOP TEN (100 pts.)

Listed below are the all-time top ten fighters in each division, based upon a consensus of several experts' rankings and fans' polls. Name your own top ten and see how close you come to the official ratings.

1. *Heavyweights*: Corbett, Fitzsimmons, Jeffries, Johnson, Dempsey, Tunney, Louis, Marciano, Ali, Frazier
2. *Light-Heavyweights*: Fitzsimmons, McCoy, O'Brien, Dillon, Berlenbach, Delaney, Loughran, Conn, Moore, Foster
3. *Middleweights*: Fitzsimmons, Ryan, M. Gibbons, Ketchel, Greb, Walker, Papke, Cerdan, Zale, Robinson
4. *Welterweights*: M. B. Smith, Walcott, Ted Kid Lewis, Britton, McLarnin, Ross, Armstrong, Robinson, Griffith, Napoles
5. *Lightweights*: Lavigne, Gans, Nelson, Ritchie, Welsh, Leonard, Canzoneri, Armstrong, Brown, Ortiz
6. *Featherweights*: Griffo, McGovern, Atell, Kilbane, Driscoll, J. Dundee, Chocolate, Armstrong, Pep, Saddler
7. *Bantamweights*: Dixon, Coulon, Williams, Herman, J. Lynch, Brown, Escobar, Ortiz, Jofre, Olivares
8. *Flyweights*: Wilde, Villa, Buff, LaBarba, Wolgast, Genaro, B. Lynch, Kane, Perez (only 9)
9. In the above polls, Fitzsimmons and Armstrong are each listed in three divisions. Who has the best cumulative rating in the consensus poll?
10. Who is most often selected as the best pound-for-pound boxer in the sport's history?

98. THE MUHAMMAD ALI SUPER QUIZ I (15 pts.)

How well do you remember brash Cassius's early years?

1. What was Ali's first exposure to the boxing world?
2. How old was he?
3. Who was his early trainer?
4. When did Ali first box on TV?
5. Who was the black trainer Ali worked with as an amateur?
6. How many amateur bouts did Ali lose?
7. Who handed Ali his last amateur defeat?
8. *True or False*: As a student, Ali was in the bottom of his class.
9. In which weight division did Ali win his Olympic gold medal?
10. Why was his gold medal won in that weight class?
11. What amateur nemesis did Ali meet in the Olympic semi-finals?
12. *True or False*: Ali acted patriotically during the Olympic Games.
13. What kind of professional contract did Ali sign?
14. How many pro bouts did Ali have before coming under Angelo Dundee's tutelage?
15. When did Ali first meet Dundee?

99. MUHAMMAD ALI SUPER QUIZ II (15 pts.)

Chart the dancing master's rise to the top of the heavyweight division.

1. Which heavyweight champ did Ali spar with in 1961?
2. When did Ali make his first prediction?
3. What meeting outside the ring influenced Ali's later flamboyance?
4. Against whom did he make his first Madison Square Garden appearance?
5. In which bout was Ali actually trailing on points when his opponent had to retire due to a cut?
6. Which of Ali's opponents was defeated overwhelmingly, had one more bout two months later, and then went into a coma and eventually died?
7. Who was the first ex-champ Ali met in the ring?
8. When did Ali begin his association with Drew "Bundini" Brown?
9. Which of Ali's early bouts brought cries of fix from the crowd?
10. Who floored Ali the second time?
11. What was Ali's condition after round four in his first bout with Sonny Liston?
12. How long after winning the title did it take Ali to adopt his Muslim name?
13. Who introduced Ali to the United Nations?
14. What was controversial about the second Ali-Liston bout?
15. Why did Ali lose popularity after the Patterson bout?

100. MUHAMMAD ALI SUPER QUIZ III (20 pts.)

Climb back into the ring with Ali as he begins his second reign as heavyweight champion of the world.

1. What was so unusual about Ali's second fight with George Chuvalo?
2. What southpaw gave Ali a lot of trouble?
3. Who first took the title from Ali?
4. What did Ali do to the W.B.A. "champ," Ernie Terrell?
5. What was Ali's last bout before his forced retirement?
6. What national magazine maintained Ali was still champ when others took the title from him?
7. How much time expired between Ali's draft refusal and his eventual exoneration by the Supreme Court?
8. Who did Ali meet in his first bout after retirement?
9. What was his only other tune-up fight before meeting Frazier?
10. What was unusual about the first Frazier-Ali bout?
11. How many rounds did light-heavy king Bob Foster last with Ali?
12. Only once did Ali go more than two straight bouts without a KO. When?
13. In what city did Ali suffer a broken-jaw loss to surprising Ken Norton?
14. What was the location of the three Ali-Frazier bouts?
15. Who knocked Ali down the third time?
16. Who knocked Ali down the fourth time?
17. Who led Ali on points going into the eleventh round before the champ turned on the juice to stop his gutsy foe and regain the title?
18. Besides Frazier, what boxers have fought Ali twice?
19. Did an Ali injury ever force postponement of a bout?
20. What else do you know about Ali?—the night Dundee was not in his corner? the first prediction he missed? his first wife's name? his childrens' names? his largest paycheck? etc.?

ANSWER SECTION

1. SENDING THE CROWD HOME EARLY

1. Tommy Burns
2. Young Corbett III
3. Joe Gans
4. Ted Kid Lewis
5. George Chip
6. Joe King Roman
7. Al Singer
8. Terry McGovern
9. (b)
10. (d)

2. THIRD MAN IN THE RING

1. Tex Rickard
2. Arthur Donavon
3. Tony Perez
4. Tony Perez
5. Ruby Goldstein
6. Dave Barry
7. Billy Cavanagh
8. Ruby Goldstein
9. Wyatt Earp
10. Harry Ertle
11. Jimmy Crowley
12. The first round bell rang as referee Pecord tolled "seven" over the fallen champion. Dempsey, who had already exited the ring, was called back by his manager Doc Kearns to continue the slaughter.
13. Jersey Joe Walcott
14. Ruby Goldstein
15. Jack Smith

3. FIGHT SITES

1. Jack Dempsey KO'd light-heavyweight champ Georges Carpentier in fourth round of "Battle of the Century" to retain heavyweight title
2. Jess Willard KO'd Jack Johnson in twenty-sixth round to capture heavyweight
3. Gene Tunney outpointed former champion Jack Dempsey over ten rounds in "Battle of the Long Count" to retain heavyweight crown
4. Heavy underdog Jack Dempsey pulverized champ Jess Willard in three-round TKO to win heavyweight title
5. Jack Johnson easily stopped Tommy Burns in fourteenth round to become first black heavyweight champion
6. George Foreman TKO'd Joe Frazier in second round to claim heavyweight championship of the world
7. Bob Fitzsimmons deflated champion James J. Corbett with solar plexus knockout blow in fourteenth round to win heavyweight title

ANSWERS / 93

8. Jack Dempsey outpointed challenger Tommy Gibbons (and bankrupted the town of Shelby) over fifteen rounds to retain heavyweight title
9. Black champion Jack Johnson permanently retired ex-titleholder James J. Jeffries with fifteen-round TKO victory
10. Muhammad Ali regained heavyweight title by kayoing George Foreman in eighth round
11. Champion John L. Sullivan stopped challenger Jake Kilrain in seventy-fifth round to retain heavyweight title
12. Challenger Gene Tunney dethroned rusty champ Jack Dempsey in ten-round decision
13. James J. Corbett outboxed champion John L. Sullivan in twenty-one-round KO victory
14. James J. Braddock scored major upset by outpointing champ Max Baer to win heavyweight crown
15. Champion George Foreman destroyed Ken Norton in two-round KO victory

4. THE GREAT WHITE HOPES

1. Jack Johnson, who was dismissed by many bigoted whites as being an "uppity nigger"
2. Jess Willard, who took the title from Johnson on a 26th round KO in 1915
3. Georges Carpentier claimed the "White Hope" title after beating Gunboat Smith. He later lost a title bout to world champion Jack Dempsey
4. Frank Moran
5. Fred Fulton
6. Luther McCarty, who was knocked out by Arthur Pelkey in the first round of their tragic bout. The autopsy revealed that McCarty actually died as a result of being kicked in the head by a horse a couple of weeks before the fight
7. Jim Flynn
8. Gunboat Smith
9. Carl Morris
10. Luther McCarty

5. COUNTING FOR THE KNOCKDOWNS

1. Battling Nelson (down 7 times) vs. Christy Williams (down 42 times)—49 total knockdowns in 17 rounds
2. Joe Jeanette (down 27 times) vs. Sam McVey (down 11 times)—38 knockdowns in a 49-round KO for Jeanette
3. Christy Williams, downed 42 times by Battling Nelson in 1902 and Jack Havlin, by Tommy Warren in 1888
4. Joe Jeanette was knocked down by Sam McVey 27 times but still managed to win the fight
5. Joe Grim
6. Battling Nelson—vs. Christy Williams (see no. 3 above), vs. Joe Headmark (down 5 times) Nelson (down 17 times), and vs. Harry Griffin (down 13 times) Nelson (no knockdowns)
7. Bantamweight Vic Towell floored Danny O'Sullivan 14 times en route to a ten-

round KO victory on December 2, 1950
8. Jack Dempsey (down 2 times) vs. Luis Firpo (down 9 times), September 14, 1923
9. Round one of the above-mentioned Dempsey (down 2 times) vs. Firpo (down 7 times) bout
10. Round five of the Towell vs. Sullivan bantamweight title bout. O'Sullivan knocked his opponent down eight times in the round

6. THE FRIDAY-NIGHT FIGHTS

1. 10 p.m. (E.S.T.)
2. Russ Hodges
3. Jack Drees
4. Dr. Joyce Brothers, whose extensive knowledge of boxing earned her the grand prize on *The $64,000 Question*
5. Jimmy Powers
6. Bill
7. Bill Nimmo
8. Don Dunphy, the dean of boxing announcers
9. Saturday
10. Gillette (The Gillette Cavalcade of Sports is on the air!!)

7. BELOW THE BELT

1. Max Schmeling
2. Tom Sharkey, who won by foul over Fitzsimmons in eight rounds on December 2, 1896 and over Corbett in nine rounds on November 22, 1898
3. Roberto Duran
4. Jack Britton
5. Joe Louis, who retained his title when challenger Buddy Baer was disqualified in the seventh round of their 1941 match
6. Joe Gans
7. Battling Siki
8. Willie Ritchie
9. Jackie Fields
10. (f)

8. ...EIGHT, NINE, TEN—YER OUT!

1. John Henry Lewis
2. Third
3. Carlos Monzon
4. The sixth round
5. Tommy Ryan
6. Joey Maxim
7. Battling Nelson
8. Louis kayoed all five in title bouts
9. Bob Montgomery
10. Jimmy Wilde

9. BROTHER WARRIORS

1. (f) 6. (c)
2. (d) 7. (h)
3. (a) 8. (i)
4. (b) 9. (g)
5. (j) 10. (e)

10. MILLION DOLLAR GATES

1. Dempsey vs. Carpentier, Jersey City, July 2, 1921
2. The second Tunney-Dempsey bout at Soldier's Field, Chicago on September 22, 1927 ($2,658,660)
3. The first Ali-Frazier bout at Madison Square Garden on March 8, 1971
4. Tony Zale vs. Billy Pryor on August 16, 1941
5. Henry Armstrong vs. Frizie Zivic on January 17, 1941 at Madison Square Garden (23,306)
6. George Foreman and Muhammad Ali each received five million dollars for their October 30, 1974 bout in Zaire, Africa
7. The Ali-Foreman bout
8. Jack Dempsey, against Tunney (1926), Sharkey (1927) and Tunney again in a return match (1927)
9. Dempsey vs. Tommy Gibbons, July 4, 1923 in Shelby Montana. The town went broke
10. Joe Louis, against Baer, Schmeling (2nd fight), and Conn (2nd fight)

11. RING ALIASES

1. Jersey Joe Walcott
2. Battling Siki
3. Young Griffo
4. Joe Louis
5. Sugar Ray Robinson
6. Battling Nelson
7. Henry Armstrong
8. Jack Sharkey
9. Beau Jack
10. Young Zulu Kid
11. Tommy Burns
12. Benny Leonard
13. Rocky Graziano
14. Jackie Fields
15. Ted Kid Lewis

12. THE GREAT JOHN L.

1. "The Boston Strong Boy"

2. Lawrence
3. Professor John Donaldson
4. Paddy Ryan
5. Charley Mitchell
6. (a)
7. Patsy Cardiff
8. Jake Kilrain
9. True
10. William Muldoon

13. GENTLEMAN JIM

1. He was a San Francisco bank teller
2. The left hook
3. Joe Choynski
4. Jake Kilrain
5. Corbett knocked out Mitchell in the third round
6. Peter Courtney
7. Corbett, by a knockout
8. The fourteenth round
9. The twenty-third round
10. Corbett knocked out Kid McCoy in the ninth round on August 30, 1900

14. RUBY ROBERT

1. True
2. Heavyweight, light-heavyweight, and middleweight
3. Jack Dempsey, the Nonpareil
4. Ron Riordan
5. Peter Maher
6. He was knocked out by James J. Jeffries in the eleventh round of his first title defense
7. Fale. Fitz never fought Burns
8. The light-heavyweight class
9. True
10. At Bob's championship bout against heavyweight titleholder James J. Corbett on March 17, 1897 in Carson City, Nevada. He followed his wife's advice and the rest is now history

15. THE BOILERMAKER

1. (b)
2. Joe Choynski
3. Peter Jackson
4. The eleventh round
5. Tom Sharkey
6. False. Jeffries KO'd Corbett twice, but needed twenty-three rounds in 1900 and ten rounds in 1903 to accomplish this creditable feat

7. No one. Jeffries retired as undefeated heavyweight champion of the world
8. He was TKO'd by Johnson in the fifteenth round when his handlers threw in the towel
9. Three times
10. True

16. TINY TOMMY

1. Marvin Hart
2. Philadelphia Jack O'Brien
3. Joe Beckett, who knocked out Burns in the latter's final professional fight (non-title)
4. Eleven times
5. Bill Squires
6. The light-heavyweight title. Since both fighters were under the heavyweight class weight minimum, Burns had actually dethroned Philadelphia Jack as light-heavy king while retaining his own crown. Fortunately for O'Brien, however, Burns did not want his title
7. True
8. (d) Kelly fought two draws with Burns
9. True
10. False. Police stopped the fight in the fourteenth round with both men standing on their feet. Johnson was declared the victor and new heavyweight champion of the world

17. L'IL ARTHUR

1. Jack Johnson won a fifteen-round decision over Langford after being knocked down in the seventh round
2. True
3. Bob Fitzsimmons
4. Tommy Burns
5. Stanley Ketchel
6. Six times
7. Frank Moran
8. Mann Act violation—interestate transportation of a white woman for immoral purposes
9. (e)
10. Three: Etta Duryea Johnson, Lucille Cameron Johnson, and Irene Pineau Johnson

18. THE MANASSA MAULER

1. Kid Blackie
2. "Fireman" Jim Flynn, who scored four knockdowns enroute to a first-round KO victory in Murray, Utah on February 13, 1917
3. Dempsey needed only 18 and 14 seconds to kayo Fulton and Morris respectively

98 / The World Championship Boxing Quizbook

4. Willard quit on his stool after the third round
5. Four rounds
6. Nine times, including the final trip to the canvas on which Firpo was counted out
7. False. Dempsey decisioned slick-boxing Tommy Gibbons over fifteen rounds
8. Jack Sharkey, who exposed his jaw to Dempsey while turning to the referee to complain about an alleged low blow
9. The seventh round
10. Clarence "Cowboy" Luttrell. Dempsey scored a KO victory in the second round

19. THE FIGHTING MARINE

1. Harry Greb, on a fifteen-round decision
2. Battling Levinsky
3. May 23, 1922—Lost fifteen-round decision, February 23, 1923—Won fifteen-round decision, December 10, 1923—Won fifteen-round decision, September 17, 1924—No decision, March 27, 1925—No decision
4. False. Tunney regained the title by outpointing Harry Greb over fifteen rounds
5. Fifteen rounds
6. Tommy Gibbons
7. Twice
8. False. It rained cats-and-dogs during their first set-to
9. True
10. Tom Heeney

20. THE BOSTON GOB

1. Sharkey won by foul when referee Patsy Haley disqualified Wills for failing to put up a decent fight
2. Jack Delaney
3. (1) (d), (2) (b), (3) (a), (4) (e), (5) (c)
4. The fourth round
5. True
6. He won a fifteen-round decision
7. Sharkey lost his title in his first defense
8. Primo Carnera
9. A right uppercut (which many observers never saw)
10. Joe Louis

21. THE LIVERMORE LARRUPER

1. Frankie Campbell
2. Tom Heeney, who Baer stopped in three rounds on January 16, 1931
3. Paulino Uzcudun
4. Max Schmeling
5. The Star of David
6. Primo Carnera
7. Baer never recorded a successful title defense. He lost his crown on his first outing against James J. Braddock

8. (c)
9. Lou Nova
10. Jethro Bodine, in *The Beverly Hillbillies*

22. THE BROWN BOMBER

1. Primo Carnera. Joe TKO'd "da Preem" in the sixth round
2. James J. Braddock
3. Louis had to give up ten percent of his earnings for the next ten years to get the title shot
4. True—Primo Carnera (1935), Max Baer (1935), Max Schmeling (1936 and 1938), Jack Sharkey (1936), James J. Braddock (1937), Jersey Joe Walcott (1947 and 1948), Ezzard Charles (1950), and Rocky Marciano (1951)
5. Tommy Farr
6. "The Bum of the Month Club"
7. 2:04 seconds of the first round. Louis smashed his German foe to the canvas three times
8. Buddy lost in seven rounds via disqualification to Louis on May 23, 1941 and was kayoed in one round by Joe on January 9, 1942. Brother Max was knocked out by Louis in four rounds on September 24, 1935
9. Max Schmeling twice, James J. Braddock, Tony Galento, Buddy Baer, Jersey Joe Walcott twice, and Rocky Marciano
10. Wendell Wilkie, Republican candidate for President
11. Jersey Joe Walcott
12. Twenty-five times, also a record
13. Three. He was knocked out by Max Schmeling in twelve rounds on June 19, 1936, outpointed by Ezzard Charles on September 27, 1950, and kayoed by Rocky Marciano in the eighth round of his last fight on October 26, 1951

23. THE BROCKTON BLOCKBUSTER

1. (c)
2. True
3. Eight rounds
4. The thirteenth round
5. One round
6. False. Rocky decisioned Charles in a hard-fought bout on June 17, 1954 and knocked out Ezz in eight frames on September 17, 1954
7. Six times
8. Archie Moore
9. Twice, in the first round of his 1952 title fight with Jersey Joe Walcott and again in the second round of his 1955 clash with Archie Moore
10. Coley Wallace

24. THE RABBIT

1. True
2. Sixteen times

100 / The World Championship Boxing Quizbook

3. Patterson KO'd big Tom McNeely in four rounds on December 4, 1961 in Toronto, Canada
4. Seven times
5. Pete Rademacher, who had Floyd on the cnavas prior to his being knocked out in the sixth round
6. The fifth round
7. True
8. Sonny needed only four more seconds to dispose of his vulnerable quarry, knocking Floyd senseless in 2:10 seconds of round one
9. Jimmy Ellis
10. Muhammad Ali

25. THE UGLY BEAR

1. Charles
2. Marty Marshall
3. Cleveland Williams
4. (e) Liston decisioned Machen over twelve rounds on September 7, 1960
5. Cassius Clay
6. True
7. He claimed to have suffered a shoulder injury
8. The first round
9. Leotis Martin, in the ninth round of their December 6, 1969 match
10. Chuck Wepner

26. SMOKIN' JOE

1. Cloverlay
2. Oscar Bonavena
3. George Chuvalo
4. Buster Mathis
5. False. Frazier stopped Quarry in seven rounds on June 23, 1969 and again in five rounds on June 17, 1974
6. Jimmy Ellis
7. Bob Foster
8. Six
9. The fourteenth round
10. One. Frazier downed Ali in the fifteenth round of their first match

ANSWERS / 101

27. PUGILISTIC POTPOURRI

```
B A D E G L O O Z N I R T E L J U T R E E M O P J
E K O I G O R O S S U F I D E W X V O L K Y U K C
P L O G R U I J E F X W I N D O N E R O M E G G Y
O R D E H I C H O P P I Y A S T L D O L E Q U I G
T R Y I J O K O U Z A L E T R U K I O O S P U G H
H I K I M W A T T R E L O P L U D L E X U V E T Y
O U J I P A R E T Y E S H U T R O L I B L I F F O
Y I C K E D D O O F E G R I Q U N O J E L E E V S
I R F O J E R B L E S K I C A L I N U T I M E S T
P Y R I H E D D O L P E X E C R I G K O V E S K Y
O F E W A L C O T T I D E M I X I F O Z A T E N W
R E P L O J E D I G H T C O R B E T T I N O O K E
U N G E U D O R P E M O L L U J E Q U O G O M M I
D E P O H U C R A V E D I K L O S S E W I B O V E
R I A L E N O O S T I C O P R I H E Q X O L L U M
I D P R O D E T T E C O S E L L E L O G G E W A X
J I K U R E F O R E M A N I J O R I S S I G L I B
I P E T T E D L A R T O K S T R I B L I N G E P U
W I F O O L O N N I K E F O H I C K O M E Z I J E
O G U K E M C C O Y E D D I G O L E M I W U F F O
P R I H O L L D E S H O M F P R I T U N N E Y I X
O F R A Z I E R O O H E D I J O N N E F I Q U A B
L I F L A D E Y O K O B B E W G H I R Y O P E G G
O D E H I K K O S E T R I N O R T O N E S F I L E
Q U O L E G G O U S H E T H O M M E W A F U G R E
```

28. IN THIS CORNER...: PHOTO QUIZ I

1. Maxie Rosenbloom
2. Joe Brown
3. Max Schmeling
4. Rocky Graziano
5. Jack Johnson
6. Benny Leonard
7. Georges Carpentier
8. Tony Zale
9. Terry McGovern
10. Marvin Hart

29. BARE KNUCKLERS

1. (c)
2. (f)
3. (e)
4. (g)
5. (l)
6. (d)
7. (a)
8. (b)
9. (i)
10. (h)
11. (n)
12. (j)
13. (o)
14. (k)
15. (m)

30. RULES OF THE GAME

1. (f)
2. (g)
3. (a)
4. (b)
5. (c)
6. (j)
7. (e)
8. (h)
9. (i)
10. (d)

31. THE DOUGHBOYS RETURN

1. (f)
2. (h)
3. (j)
4. (g)
5. (a)
6. (b)
7. (i)
8. (d)
9. (c)
10. (e)

32. GOING THE DISTANCE

1. Barney Ross
2. False. He lost his fourth and final middleweight title to Paul Pender, not Bobo Olson
3. Johnny Kilbane
4. The featherweight title
5. (e) Ali TKO'd Bonavena in the fifteenth round of their December 7, 1970 match
6. Ezzard Charles
7. Archie Moore
8. False. Carnera decisioned Uzcudun and Tommy Loughran in defense of his title
9. Jack Dillon
10. Pete Latzo

33. WE WUZ ROBBED

1. Max Schmeling was awarded the vacant heavyweight title over Jack Sharkey after being struck by a low blow in the fourth round on June 12, 1930
2. Sharkey was "given" a home-country decision over Schmeling in New York on June 21, 1932, even though he probably lost by four rounds
3. Jersey Joe Walcott knocked Louis down in rounds one and four but lost a fifteen-round decision
4. Henry Armstrong, who lost the lightweight title to Lou Ambers
5. Referee Pep ruled the featherweight title bout between Johnny Famechon and Fighting Harada a draw. A recount of his card, however, favored Famechon 70-69. Most reporters disagreed
6. Marvin Hart won a twenty-round decision over Johnson in which the latter may have loafed or, as he claimed in his life story, let up for fear of his life
7. Marcel Thil, versus Gorilla Jones and Lou Brouillard (twice). The Brouillard fouls were questionable
8. Robinson KO'd Gerhard Hecht in the first round (disallowed) and knocked him out in round two (disqualified for a kidney punch). The commission later ruled the bout a no-decision contest
9. Paul Pender won two fifteen-round decisions on the ballots of home-town judges, although the referee voted for Robinson each time.
10. In a three-round bout for the King's Trophy Bantam Title, Wilde was up eleven points but lost to Pal Moore—perhaps the biggest steal in boxing history!

34. TALE OF THE TAPE

1. Tommy Burns
2. Bob Fitzsimmons
3. Primo Carnera
4. Muhammad Ali
5. Jess Willard
6. Floyd Patterson
7. John L. Sullivan
8. Jack Dempsey
9. Rocky Marciano
10. Jack Johnson

35. BOXING PECULIARITIES

1. (g)
2. (d)
3. (i)
4. (a)
5. (f)
6. (b)
7. (j)
8. (e)
9. (c)
10. (h)

36. THE NEAR-CHAMPS

1. Jack Munroe, who was later kayoed in two rounds by Jeffries
2. Jim Johnson
3. Peter Maher, who Fitzsimmons beat before meeting Corbett
4. Ernie Terrell
5. Peter Jackson
6. Tom Sharkey
7. Philadelphia Jack O'Brien
8. Jack Root
9. Luis Firpo
10. Ron Lyle

37. TINSEL TOWN BOXERS

1. Victor McLaglen, who won the Best Actor award for *The Informer,* lost to heavyweight king Jack Johnson in six rounds on March 10, 1909 at Vancouver, Canada
2. Paul Newman
3. Bob Hope
4. Coley Wallace

5. Jack Palance
6. *Champion*
7. Errol Flynn
8. James Earl Jones
9. Primo Carnera. Incidentally, the film co-starred Rod Steiger and Humphrey Bogart and was the latter's final screen appearance
10. *Monkey On My Back*

38. NICKNAMES I

1. Harry Greb
2. Edward Smith
3. Ace Hudkins
4. Willie Pep
5. Georges Carpentier
6. Al Davis
7. Mickey Walker
8. George Dixon
9. Tony Galento
10. Billy Petrolle
11. James J. Braddock
12. Jimmy Wilde
13. Jack La Motta
14. Joe Brown
15. Lou Ambers

39. NICKNAMES II

1. (f)
2. (e)
3. (b)
4. (i)
5. (a)
6. (g)
7. (j)
8. (c)
9. (h)
10. (d)

40. FIGHT LINGO

1. A boxer with no talent
2. A very wild puncher
3. A blow on the head
4. A free ticket
5. A hard punch
6. A boxer who gets knocked out a lot

106 / The World Championship Quizbook

7. Blood
8. A bout
9. Slow
10. A very light punch

41. THE MICHIGAN ASSASSIN

1. Stanislaus Kiecal
2. Montana
3. Joe Thomas
4. Mike Twin Sullivan
5. Jack Twin Sullivan, who was KO'd by Ketchel in the twentieth round. The Sullivan twins were born on September 23, 1878 in Cambridge, Massachusetts
6. After Billy Papke hit Ketchel instead of shaking hands with him at the beginning of their bout, the challenger proceeded to knock Stan down five times in round one en route to a lopsided twelfth-round KO victory.
7. Less than 2 months—from September 7 to November 26, 1908
8. Although Papke clearly won the fight, Ketchel was "given" a twenty-round decision by referee Red Roche to even their series at 2-2.
9. He decisioned Jack O'Brien in ten rounds and TKO'd him in three
10. Ketchel crossed up Johnson by knocking him down in round twelve. In one flowing motion, Johnson fell, came back up, hit Ketchel and knocked him out cold. Several of Ketchel's teeth were found embedded in Johnson's right glove.

42. MAMA'S BOY

1. Freddie Welsh
2. Seven times
3. False. Leonard retired as undefeated world lightweight champion in 1924
4. (b)
5. Seven years
6. (b)
7. Johnny Dundee
8. Lew Tendler
9. Richie Mitchell
10. Jimmy McLarnin

43. SUGAR RAY

1. Walker Smith
2. Madison Square Garden
4. The welterweight title
5. Jake LaMotta
6. Five times—1951, 1951-52, 1955-57, 1957, 1958-60. He was retired from 1952-1955
7. By the heat. He collapsed from the scorching 104 degree heat in his bid to wrest the light-heavy title from Joey Maxim on June 25, 1952. The Sugar Man was

comfortably ahead on points at the time. Robinson temporarily retired for two years after the bout
8. Randy Turpin, Gene Fullmer, and Carmen Basilio
9. Paul Pender won two split-decisions over Sugar Ray in his home-town of Boston. The referee voted for Robinson in each bout.
10. Surprisingly not! He had four wins (three by KO), five losses, and one draw in title bouts. In his total career, Robinson lost only three times in twleve years before retiring—to Jack La Motta, Randy Turpin and Joey Maxim, but was defeated sixteen times in ten years after his return to ring action

44. THE OLD MONGOOSE

1. Twice. He lost by a knockout to Rocky Marciano in 1955 and again to Floyd Patterson in 1956
2. Jack "Doc" Kearns, who guided Jack Dempsey to the world championship
3. Turtle shell
4. Ezzard Charles
5. (d)
6. Nine times
7. True
8. Yvon Durelle
9. He was TKO'd in the fourth round
10. Carl Bobo Olson
11. The ninth round
12. The New York Athletic Commission and the European Boxing Union, for failing to defend his title against top contender Harold Johnson

45. THE BOSTON TAR BABY

1. He was a black boxer who started his boxing career in Boston
2. Joe Gans, on a fifteen-round decision
3. Joe Walcott, who fought Sam to a fifteen-round draw (even tough Langford won more rounds) and The Dixie Kid, who Langford KO'd twice
4. Stanley Ketchel battled Langford to a six-round stalemate, even though ring observers thought the latter had won the fight
5. Philadelphia Jack O'Brien, by a KO in five rounds
6. Only Gans and O'Brien were champs when they met Langford. Gans insisted that Langford come into the fight over the weight limit to protect his title in the event of a loss. O'Brien remained champion by popular acclaim even though Langford beat him
7. Johnson claimed people would not want to see two blacks fight for the title
8. Harry Wills, who fought Langford twenty-three times. Langford won more often, even though Wills was early in his career and in better condition
9. Sam McVey (15), Joe Jeanette (14), Jim Barry (12), and Jeff Clarke (11)
10. Fred Fulton forced Langford to quit after seven rounds with a permanently-damaged optic nerve. This injury led to his later blindness

46. HAMMERIN' HANK

1. True
2. Featherweight, lightweight, and welterweight
3. One. He was knocked out in three rounds by Al Iovino
4. Baby Arizmendi
5. Petey Sarron
6. Barney Ross
7. (e)
8. Fritzie Zivic
9. Lou Ambers
10. (a)
11. Lou Ambers
10. (a)
11. Lou Ambers, by a unanimous decision
12. Fritzie Zivic
13. Ceferino Garcia
14. (e)
15. He became a Baptist preacher

47. THE TOY BULLDOG

1. No. He lost to Jack Britton
2. He avenged his loss to Britton by winning the title, November 1, 1922 on a fifteen-round decision
3. False. He went 2½ years without a defense and lost the title in only his third defense of the crown
4. Pete Latzo
5. False. He lost to Harry Greb
6. Tiger Flowers, on December 3, 1926, in a fifteen-round decision
7. He gave it up due to increased weight after 4½ years
8. Yes, but he lost twice to Tommy Loughran and to Maxie Rosenbloom
9. Yes, though often outweighed by thirty pounds or more
10. He lost two eight-round TKOs—to Joe Dundee, having entered the bout with plaster over a cut left eye, and to Max Schmeling, who floored him three times

48. THE UNKNOWN TRIPLE-CHAMP

1. In Slidell, Louisiana on November 6, 1908
2. No. He fought a ten-round draw with N.B.A. bantamweight champion Bud Taylor
3. The featherweight crown, on a fifteen-round decision over Benny Bass
4. False. He lost the title to Andre Routis on a fifteen-round decision in his first defense just seven months later
5. The lightweight and junior-welterweight titles
6. They were the only two boxers to fight for the title in four different weight divisions. Canzoneri failed in his try for the bantam crown, settling for the featherweight, lightweight and junior-welterweight titles
7. (1)He lost two titles in one bout—the lightweight and junior-welterweight crowns;

(2) It was only a ten-round bout;
(3) It was a split-decision
8. (a), 11 wins, 9 losses, and 1 draw
9. False. Tony won only two by KO
10. Only once, in his last of 181 bouts

49. FISTIC FIRSTS

1. Zack Clayton, Walcott vs. Charles (1952)
2. Pat Barlow (1975)
3. George Dixon, the bantamweight title
4. Battling Siki
5. George Dixon, the featherweight title
6. Ted Kid Lewis, to protect his lips from his uneven teeth, against Phil Bloom in 1914
7. James J. Corbett
8. Bill Richmond and Tom Molineaux, both black
9. Tommy Burns, against Gunner Moir in London (1907). Burns KO'd Moir in the tenth round
10. James J. Corbett

50. RETURN OF THE CHAMPION

1. Lost. He was actually still considered champ when he returned but lost the title to Bob Fitzsimmons and failed to regain the crown against Jim Jeffries
2. Lost to Jack Johnson
3. Lost to Ezzard Charles
4. Re-won the title four times
5. No title shot
6. No title shot
7. Re-won the N.B.A. lightweight title in bout with Slugger White
8. Re-won the featherweight title from Johnny Famechon
9. Lost to Battling Battalino and Kid Chocolate in featherweight title contests (LaBarba was previously a flyweight)
10. Re-won W.B.C. featherweight title from Jose Legra. Since he was previously a bantamweight, Jofre is the only fighter to come back and win a boxing title in a heavier weight class

51. WILL THE REAL WORLD CHAMPIONS PLEASE STAND UP?

1. Tom Sharkey
2. Leo Lomski
3. Ace Hudkins
4. Stan Hayward
5. Ceferino Garcia
6. Frankie Klick
7. Art Aragon

8. Eddie Cannonball Martin
9. Young Griffo
10. Frankie Burns
11. Small Montana

52. OLYMPIC CHAMPIONS

1. Nine
2. The middleweight division
3. False. Clay won the gold medal as a light-heavyweight
4. Teofilio Stevenson
5. Pete Rademacher
6. Hungarian southpaw Laszlo Papp, who never lost a professional fight
7. Ingemar Johansson, representing Sweden at the 1952 Olympic Games
8. Three
9. O.L. Kirk, who won gold medals for both the bantamweight and featherweight divisions at the 1904 Games in St. Louis, Missouri
10. Floyd Patterson
11. (d)
12. Mexico City
13. False. Smokin' Joe won his gold medal at the Tokyo Games in 1964
14. Jackie Fields, who won his gold medal at Paris in 1924
15. Sugar Ray Seales, who won in the lightweight division

53. PICK THE DECADE

1. 1960's
2. 1930's
3. 1880's
4. 1940's
5. 1910's
6. 1890's
7. 1950's
8. 1970's
9. 1900's
10. 1920's

54. HOME TOWN BOYS I

1. (b)
2. (h)
3. (f)
4. (c)
5. (m)
6. (e)
7. (l)
8. (n)

9. (a)
10. (o)
11. (d)
12. (g)
13. (i)
14. (j)
15. (k)

55. HOME TOWN BOYS II

1. (f)
2. (a)
3. (b)
4. (c)
5. (d)
6. (j)
7. (e)
8. (g)
9. (i)
10. (h)

56. MAIN EVENTS: PHOTO QUIZ II

1. Fourteen times
2. Jimmy McLarnin
3. Carmen Basilio
4. False. Papke decisioned Moreau over 16 rounds
5. Four times
6. On June, 1952, Sugar Ray fell victim to the blistering outdoor heat and lost his bid to wrest the light-heavyweight title from champ Joey Maxim (Robinson was far ahead on points at the time). Maxim lost the title in his next outing to challenger Moore. Had Sugar Ray survived the heat against Maxim, he probably would have Moore in a title defense
7. A left-hook
8. Three
9. Stan Ketchel
10. False. Johnson was champion at the time of their bout
11. Only two, to Joe Frazier and Ken Norton
12. The welterweight championship
13. Only one, Tom Heeney
14. Jack Johnson
15. Tex Rickard
16. Dick Tiger
17. False. Louis was a 4-1 favorite
18. Johnny Wilson
19. Marciano "kayoed" Ali in the thirteenth round
20. True
21. Twenty-four years old

22. False. Walker never fought for the heavyweight title
23. The featherweight division
24. Only once, before moving up to a heavier weight class

57. RING DEATHS

1. Jimmy Doyle, KO'd in eight by Sugar Ray Robinson
2. Benny Paret, TKO'd in twelve by Emile Griffith
3. Davey Moore, TKO'd in ten by Sugar Ramos
4. Sam Baroudi, KO'd in ten by Ezzard Charles
5. Frankie Campbell, KO'd in five by Max Baer
6. Ernie Schaaf, KO'd in thirteen by Primo Carnera after suffering injuries in a ten-round decision loss to Max Baer. This marked the second time Baer had contributed to the death of a fighter in the ring
7. Pancho Villa, in a ten-round decision loss to Jimmy McLarnin
8. Tiger Flowers KO'd Leo Gates in four rounds on November 12, 1927, but died four days later after an eye operation
9. Joe Bugner won an eight-round decision over Ulric Regis on March 11, 1969. Regis died four days later following brain surgery
10. Jimmy Barry won the bantamweight title on a twenty-round KO over Walter Croot in 1897. Croot died after the fight from injuries

58. BOXER VS. SLUGGER

1. Corbett, by a twenty-one round KO
2. Tunney, on two ten-round decisions
3. Louis, by thirteen and eight-round knockouts
4. Louis, by a KO in eight rounds
5. Ali, by seven and first-round knockouts
6. Ali, who won a twelve-round decision and a fourteenth-round TKO victory after suffering a fifteen-round decision loss in their first encounter
7. Ketchel, with a ten-round decision and a TKO in the third round
8. Greb, on a close win over fifteen rounds
9. Each won a fifteen-round decision
10. Saddler won three out of four by KOs in four, eight, and nine rounds. He lost to Pep only once on a fifteen-round decision

Boxers win 5 to 4 with 1 even, although many of the boxers were past their peak at the time of these matches.

59. SPOT THE DIVISION

1. Flyweights, with 40%. Heavyweights are far out in front at 70%.
2. Light-heavies, with 21% KOs, and welterweights, with 22% KOs, usually move up to challenge heavyweights and middle-weights respectively
3. The middleweight division
4. The lightweight division
5. The light-heavies and flyweights

ANSWERS / 113

6. The light-heavyweight division was born when Jack Root could no longer make middleweight. His manager, Lou Houseman, promoted a division between the middles and the heavies and it caught on fast. Root won the first 175-pound title
7. The welterweight (raised only from 145 to 147 in this century) and the lightweight (raised from 133 to 135 in this century)
8. The lightweights. John Moneghan first claimed the title in 1855
9. The heavyweight division with three—Jeffries, Marciano and Ali. It leads the bantamweight class with two—Jimmy Carruthers and Jimmy Barry. Jeffries, Ali and Carruthers all lost bouts, however, after coming out of retirement.
10. Bantamweight, 16% draws. Welterweights are next at 13%

60. THE HEAVYWEIGHTS

1. Only one, Floyd Patterson. Muhammad Ali never lost his title in the ring. He was stripped of his title for refusing induction into the Armed Forces
2. Jack Sharkey, who was kayoed by Dempsey in seven rounds on July 21, 1927 and stopped by Louis in three frames on August 18, 1936
3. Ezzard Charles, who lost twenty-five fights
4. Gene Tunney, Rocky Marciano, and Muhammad Ali
5. Jack Root
6. Tunney, Schmeling, Sharkey, Carnera, Baer, Braddock, Louis
7. Bob Fitzsimmons, who lost the heavyweight title to James J. Jeffries on an eleventh-round knockout in 1899 and won the light-heavyweight title by outpointing George Gardner in 1903
8. Louis Angel Firpo, who succumbed to Dempsey's ninth and final knockdown in the second round of their explosive September 14, 1923 bout
9. Jersey Joe Walcott
10. Only four times—Tommy Burns defeated Marvin Hart (February 23, 1906, twenty rounds), Gene Tunney outpointed Jack Dempsey (September 23, 1926, ten rounds), Jack Sharkey edged Max Schmeling (June 21, 1932, fifteen rounds), and James J. Braddock outboxed Max Baer (June 13, 1935, fifteen rounds)
11. Primo Carnera, who racked up 66 KO's
12. George Foreman, who knocked out 91% of the opponents he faced (through 1975). Marciano was second at 88%
13. Rocky Marciano, with 100%. He was never defeated in a professional bout
14. Jack Johnson, who appeared in 113 bouts
15. Joe Louis, who dominated the heavyweight division for over eleven years

61. THE LIGHT-HEAVIES

1. 175 pounds
2. Jack Root
3. Slapsie Maxie Rosenbloom, 289 bouts
4. Jack Dillon, 94%
5. Bob Foster, 72%
6. Archie Moore, ten years; O'Brien was second with seven years
7. Archie Moore, fourteen defenses; Foster was second with twelve
8. No

9. None. Fitzsimmons reversed the trend, becoming light-heavy champ after he was heavyweight king
10. Jack O'Brien vs. Tommy Burns (twice), Georges Carpentier vs. Jack Dempsey, Tommy Loughran vs. Primo Carnera, John Henry Lewis vs. Joe Louis, Billy Conn vs. Joe Louis, Joey Maxim vs. Ezzard Charles, Archie Moore vs. Rocky Marciano and Floyd Patterson, Bob Foster vs. Joe Frazier. All lost

62. THE MIDDLEWEIGHTS

1. 160 pounds
2. The "Nonpareil" Jack Dempsey
3. A close one! Tommy Ryan, with 86 victories in 89 fights (omitting 20 draws and no-decisions) wound up on top with a 96.63%. Carlos Monzon, with 84 wins in 87 bouts, is second at 96.55% (ommitting 13 draws and no-decisions)
4. Stan Ketchel, 75%
5. Tommy Ryan, nine years
6. Carlos Monzon, with eleven defenses (through 1975)
7. The remarkable Harry Greb, 290 bouts
8. Yes, two did. Billy Papke reclaimed it after his victor Stan Ketchel was murdered. Robinson regained it four times, a record for all divisions
9. Yes, two did. Bob Fitzsimmons won the title from George Gardner and Dick Tiger beat Jose Torres for the crown
10. Yes. Stanley Ketchel was KO'd by Jack Johnson in the twelfth round and Bob Fitzsimmons won the title from James J. Corbett on a fourteenth-round KO

63. THE WELTERWEIGHTS

1. 147 pounds
2. Joe Walcott, who was the namesake of heavyweight king Jersey Joe (Arnold Cream) Walcott
3. Tommy Ryan, 97% (excluding twenty draws and no-decision bouts)
4. Jose Napoles, 65% (through 1975)
5. Jose Napoles, six years (1969-70, 70-75)
6. Henry Armstrong, twenty defenses in 2½ years with only one loss (1938-40)
7. Jack Briton, with over 325 bouts (1905-30)
8. Jack Britton and Ted Kid Lewis. Britton held a slight edge in the series
9. Harry and Willie Lewis
10. Tommy Ryan, Mickey Walker, Ray Robinson, Carmen Basilio, and Emile Griffith

64. THE LIGHTWEIGHTS

1. 135 pounds
2. In order of their reign: Jack McAuliffe, George Kid Lavigne, Frank Erne, Joe Gans, Battling Nelson, Ad Wolgast, Willie Ritchie, Freddy Welsh, Benny Leonard
3. Canzoneri won the title from Al Singer. He lost it to Barney Ross. Ross then gave up the title. Canzoneri regained the vacant title by beating Ambers. Canzoneri

then lost the title to Ambers, who in turn lost it to Armstrong. Ambers then won back the title from Armstrong
4. Roberto Duran, 98%—49 wins in 50 fights (through 1975). Jack McAuliffe, who is reputed to have been undefeated during his career (1884-97), was behind in at least two of his eleven draws and no-decision bouts, for at best, a 95% career win percentage
5. Duran, 80% (through 1975)
6. McAuliffe, 7¾ years, although he only defended his title twice. Benny Leonard with 7 years, 7 months is probably more legitimate
7. Joe Brown, with twelve (1957-62)
8. Leonard, 209 bouts
9. Ike Williams, N.B.A. champ in 1945, world champ from 1947-51
10. James Carter won the title three times during the years 1951-55

65. THE FEATHERWEIGHTS

1. 126 pounds
2. George Dixon
3. Terry McGovern
4. Willie Pep, 95% (1944-56)
5. Sandy Saddler, 64%
6. Johnny Kilbane, eleven years. Abe Atell is second with ten years
7. Atell, twelve defenses. Dixon was second with eight
8. Officially, Johnny Dundee with 321 recorded bouts; unofficially, George Dixon, who fought in over 800 bouts
9. Kid Chocolate (real name Eligio Sardinias)
10. Dixon, Pep, Saddler, Joey Archibald, and Vincente Saldivar

66. THE BANTAMWEIGHTS

1. 118 pounds
2. George Dixon and Terry McGovern
3. Johnny Coulon, Kid Williams, Pete Herman and Joe Lynch
4. Eder Jofre, 97% (1957-73) or Jimmy Barry, 100%, if you exclude his eleven no-decisions
5. Ruben Olivares, 83% (through 1975). Jofre is second with 76%
6. Manuel Ortiz, 7 years, 2 months during two reigns. Panama Al Brown, 6 years during one stint as champion (1929-35)
7. Manuel Ortiz, 22 defenses
8. Kid Williams, 204 bouts
9. Pete Herman, Joe Lynch, Sixto Escobar and Manuel Ortiz
10. Panama Al Brown, 5 feet 11 inches tall

67. THE FLYWEIGHTS

1. 112 pounds

2. Jimmy Wilde
3. Pancho Villa, Frankie Genaro, Emile (Spider) Pladner and Fidel La Barba
4. In order of their reign: Jackie Brown (England), Benny Lynch (Scotland), Peter Kane (England), Jackie Patterson (Scotland), Rinty Monaghan (Ireland), and Terry Allen (England)
5. Jimmy Wilde, 96.92% (excluding 10 no-decisions)
6. Pascual Perez, 62%
7. Wilde, six years six months
8. Perez, eighteen defenses
9. Midget Wolgast, 147 bouts
10. Two, Pone Kingpetch and Chartchai Chionoi

68. THE JUNIOR WEIGHT TITLES

1. Both the junior-welter and junior-lightweight titles (140 and 130 pounds respectively) were in existence in the twenties until discontinued in 1933. They were revived in 1959
2. Tony Canzoneri and Barney Ross
3. Johnny Dundee, Benny Bass and Kid Chocolate
4. The junior-middleweight division (154 pounds)
6. Only once, when Benvenuti successfully jumped to the middleweight class. The others were champs below the junior weights
7. Junior-featherweight, junior-bantamweight, and junior-flyweight
8. The junior-light-heavy and junior-flyweight divisions, in the U.S. and Italy respectively
9. Nicolino Loche, who was stopped only once in 129 bouts
10. Flash Elorde

69. THE ALL-TIME GREATS

1. George Foreman, 91% (through 1975)
2. Marciano, 100%. Jimmy Barry (1891-99) also scored 100%, but had eleven no-decision bouts. Lightweight Jack McAuliffe (1884-1914) is often credited with 100, but actually trailed in two no-decision bouts
3. Joe Louis, nearly twelve years. Featherweight Johnny Kilbane with eleven years is second
4. Louis, 26 defenses. Bantam Manuel Ortiz is second with 22
5. Louis, 28. George Dixon (bantam-feather) and Henry Armstrong (feather-light-welter) each had 26
6. Dixon reputedly fought in over 800 bouts, although most are unrecorded. Jack Britton had 325 recorded bouts
7. Featherweight Willie Pep, 62 straight (1940-43) edges flyweight Salvatore Burruni with 61 straight (1960-65). Pep went on to win 73 more straight with but one draw from 1943-48. Current middleweight Carlos Monzon has not been defeated in 80 bouts (1964-75), but his string of victories has been interrupted by nine draws. Non-champ Hal Bagwell won 180 with five draws (1938-48)
8. Light-heavy Archie Moore, 141 KOs. Middleweight Ray Robinson is second with 109 KOs. Non-champ Young Stribling had 126

9. The first Ali-Frazier bout
10. Ali, by a wide margin (through 1975)
11. Maxie Rosenbloom, 187 wins. Pep is second with 164 wins
12. Eder Jofre, twelve
13. Joe Louis (1937-1950) and Sugar Ray Robinson (1946-1961)
14. Light-heavy Jack Dillon, 240 bouts. Kid Gavilan is second with 144 bouts
15. Gene Tunney, with 76. Ali is second with 51 (through 1975)

70. BATTLES OF THE CENTURY

1. Tom Cribb (white) of England beat Tom Molineaux (black) of the United States in 33 rounds, England (1810)
2. Cribb won again in eleven rounds in 1811
3. Charley Mitchell, in France
4. Jack Johnson stopped Jim Jeffries in fifteen rounds, Reno, Nevada
5. Jack Dempsey halted Georges Carpentier in four rounds, 1921, Jersey City
6. Jack Dempsey defeated Luis Firpo in two rounds, 1923, New York
7. Joe Louis annihilated Max Schmeling in one round, 1938, New York
8. March 8, 1971, New York
9. June 28, 1974, New York
10. October 1, 1975, Manila, Phillipines

71. THE CORNERMEN I

1. (f)
2. (a)
3. (e)
4. (b)
5. (h)
6. (i)
7. (c)
8. (g)
9. (j)
10. (d)

72. THE CORNERMEN II

1. (c)
2. (i)
3. (j)
4. (f)
5. (d)
6. (a)
7. (h)
8. (b)
9. (e)
10. (g)

118 / The World Championship Boxing Quizbook

73. BIG-TIME OPERATORS

1. (j)
2. (f)
3. (c)
4. (i)
5. (b)
6. (a)
7. (d)
8. (h)
9. (g)
10. (e)

74. OUTSIDE NOTABLES

1. (g)
2. (c)
3. (i)
4. (a)
5. (j)
6. (d)
7. (b)
8. (e)
9. (f)
10. (h)

75. THE BARONS OF BOXING

1. World Boxing Association
2. World Boxing Commission
3. European Boxing Union
4. National Boxing Association
5. International Boxing Union
6. Commonwealth Championships Committee
7. Japan Boxing Commission
8. New York State Athletic Commission
9. North American Boxing Federation
10. British Board of Boxing Control

76. UNSUNG GIANT-KILLERS

1. Joey Maxim
2. Florentino Fernandez
3. Benny Leonard
4. Jock Leslie
5. Jimmy McLarnin
6. Ken Buchanan

7. Tiger Flowers
8. Jim Flynn
9. Joe Beckett
10. Frankie Burns

77. BOWING OUT

1. (f)
2. (c)
3. (h)
4. (a)
5. (d)
6. (d)
7. (b)
8. (g)
9. (e)
10. (h)

78. THE FINAL COUNT

1. Heavyweight champ Sonny Liston
2. Heavyweight champ Rocky Marciano
3. Light-heavyweight champ Battling Siki
4. Heavyweight champ Ezzard Charles
5. Middleweight and light-heavyweight champ Harry Greb
6. Heavyweight, light-heavyweight, and middleweight champ Bob Fitzsimmons
7. Lightweight champ Benny Leonard
8. Heavyweight champ Jack Johnson
9. Flyweight champ Pancho Villa
10. Middleweight champ Stanley Ketchel

79. THEIR POST-GLORY YEARS I

1. (f)
2. (d)
3. (i)
4. (g)
5. (b)
6. (j)
7. (h)
8. (c)
9. (a)
10. (e)

80. THEIR POST GLORY YEARS II

1. (i)
2. (b)
3. (a)
4. (g)
5. (e)
6. (c)
7. (h)
8. (d)
9. (j)
10. (f)

81. TRADEMARKS

1. (n)
2. (h)
3. (l)
4. (c)
5. (m)
6. (e)
7. (d)
8. (k)
9. (a)
10. (g)
11. (f)
12. (i)
13. (j)
14. (o)
15. (b)

82. YOU'RE THE JUDGE

1. (e)
2. (d)
3. (a)
4. (a)
5. (a)
6. (c)
7. (c)
8. (e)
9. (b)
10. (e)

83. DIRTY FIGHTERS

1. Henry Armstrong
2. Fritzie Zivic

3. Harry Greb
4. Rocky Marciano
5. Primo Carnera
6. Billy Papke
7. Young Stribling
8. Ad Wolgast
9. Rocky Graziano
10. Mysterious Billy Smith

84. REMEMBER WHEN?..

1. (7) January 9, 1900
2. (10) July 4, 1908
3. (3) November 26, 1908
4. (9) May 11, 1922
5. (6) July 27, 1922
6. (2) August 31, 1923
7. (1) July 16, 1947
8. (8) October 29, 1948
9. (4) July 10, 1951
10. (5) June 1, 1963

85. WIN, LOSE, ... OR DRAW

1. Two. Champion Tommy Burns fought a twenty-round draw with Philadelphia Jack O'Brien on November 28, 1906 and titleholder Jack Johnson had to settle for a draw with challenger Jim Johnson in a ten-round contest on December 19, 1913
2. Peter Jackson
3. (d) Gavilan won a fifteen-round decision over Basilio to retain his welterweight title
4. Joe Choynski
5. Kid Williams
6. Charley Mitchell
7. Jack McAuliffe
8. Joe Walcott
9. (1) (b), (2) (d), (3) (a), (4) (c), (5) (e)
10. Mickey Walker

86. FIX!

1. Fixed. A plant from Sharkey's camp who was working in Corbett's corner jumped into the ring. This led to the foul call.
2. Fixed. Fitz knocked out Sharkey but referee Wyatt Earp, who had taken a bribe, called it a foul (sorry, western fans)
3. Probably fixed. Most think Gans took a dive against the lighter champ.
4. Fixed. One of two admitted fakes. LaMotta took a dive to get a later title shot.

122 / The World Championship Boxing Quizbook

5. Legitimate. Most skeptics just didn't want to believe Ali could handle Liston so easily—but the films showed he could and did.
6. Legitimate. Johnson admitted that he fabricated the confession he sold to *Ring* editor Nat Fleischer, in which he claimed to have thrown the fight.
7. Legitimate. Although Johnson may have been lazy or in fear of his life, Hart did fight very aggressively. The crowd probably affected the decision.
8. Apparently a one-man fix. Leonard hit Britton while the latter was down, thus losing by a foul. Some claim Leonard deliberately fouled Britton because he didn't want the welterweight title.
9. Probably fixed. LaBlanche knocked out Depsey with pivot blow. To protect Dempsey's title, the punch was ruled illegal, even though the blow did not violate the rules of the sport at the time the bout was fought in 1889
10. A spontaneous fix. In an apparent double knockout, the referee helped up Wolgast and counted Rivers out.

87. MEMORABLE QUOTES

1. Novelist Jack London in his post-fight coverage of the Jack Johnson—Tommy Burns title bout in Rushcutter's Bay Arena, Sydney, Australia on December 26, 1908. London was appealing to former champion James J. Jeffries to come out of retirement to recapture the heavyweight title for the white race.
2. Manager Joe Jacobs after his fighter Max Schmeling lost a controversial points decision and the heavyweight title to Jack Sharkey at New York's Long Island Bowl on June 21, 1932
3. Max Baer to Primo Carnera after both had tumbled to the canvas during the first round of their "wrestling match" in which challenger Baer "floored" "da Preem" eleven times before stopping the champ in the eleventh round, June 14, 1934
4. John L. Sullivan, last of the great bare-knuckle heavyweight champions, in just about every bar in town
5. Muhammad Ali, after watching himself get knocked out by Rocky Marciano and an NCR 315 computer in a theatrically-staged match-up
6. Joe Louis, after annihilating Max Schmeling in 2:04 seconds of the first round on June 22, 1938 to avenge his earlier knockout loss to the German challenger
7. "Two Ton" Tony Galento, rationalizing his June 28, 1939 fourth-round TKO drubbing at the hands of power-punching Joe Louis
8. Former heavyweight champion Max Baer, after being knocked out by Joe Louis in the fourth round of their September 24, 1935 title fight
9. James J. Corbett, after losing the heavyweight crown to Bob Fitzsimmons on a perfectly-timed solar plexus punch which knocked both the wind and the title from "Gentleman Jim"
10. Joe Louis, before his first ring battle with evasive Billy Conn, June 18, 1941

88. PUGILISTIC STYLES

1. (d)
2. (j)
3. (f)
4. (b)
5. (e)

6. (i)
7. (c)
8. (a)
9. (h)
10. (g)

89. PICK THE ROUND

1. Twenty-six
2. Five
3. Twelve
4. Eleven
5. Three
6. Six
7. Thirteen
8. Twenty-one
9. Thirteen
10. Seven

90. CLASSIC FIGHT SERIES

1. Sam Langford won 2, Harry Wills won 6 (15 no-decisions)
2. Ted Kid Lewis won 3, Jack Britton won 4 (12 no-decisions, 1 draw)
3. Jack Dillon won 2, Battling Levinsky won 1 (6 no-decisions, 1 draw)
4. Gene Tunney won 2, Harry Greb won 1 (2 no-decisions)
5. Pancho Villa won 6, Mike Ballerino won none (2 no-decisions, 2 draws)
6. Benny Leonard (L) and Johnny Dundee (F) fought 8 no-decision bouts
7. Joe Jeanette, who won one, Johnson won 2 (5 no-decisions, 2 draws)
8. Harold Johnson. Moore won 4 out of 5 bouts
9. Carl Bobo Olson
10. Baby Arizmendi

91. CHAMPIONSHIP REIGNS

1. Jimmy Wilde, Pancho Villa, Fidel LaBarba, Frankie Genaro, Jackie Brown, Midget Wolgast, Benny Lynch, Pascual Perez, Pone Kingpetch, Chartchai Chionoi
2. George Dixon, Johnny Coulon, Pete Herman, Joe Lynch, Charlie Phil Rosenberg, Panama Al Brown, Sixto Escobar, Manuel Ortiz, Eder Jofre, Lionel Rose
3. George Dixon, Terry McGovern, Abe Attell, Johnny Kilbane, Battling Battalino, Petey Sarron, Henry Armstrong, Willie Pep, Vincente Saldivar, Jose Legra
4. George Kid Lavigne, Joe Gans, Battling Nelson, Willie Ritchie, Sammy Mandell, Tony Canzoneri, Lou Ambers, Ike Williams, Joe Brown, Carlos Ortiz
5. Mysterious Billy Smith, Ted Kid Lewis, Pete Latzo, Jimmy McLarnin, Barney Ross, Henry Armstrong, Sugar Ray Robinson, Kid Gavilan, Carmen Basilio, Emile Griffith

6. Stanley Ketchel, Al McCoy, Johnny Wilson, Harry Greb, Tiger Flowers, Mickey Walker, Marcel Thil, Tony Zale, Jake LaMotta, Nino Benvenuti
7. Jack Dillon, Georges Carpentier, Tommy Loughran, Maxie Rosenbloom, John Henry Lewis, Billy Conn, Gus Lesnevich, Joey Maxim, Archie Moore, Jose Torres
8. James J. Jeffries, Marvin Hart, Jack Johnson, Jess Willard, Jack Dempsey, Primo Carnera, Joe Louis, Ezzard Charles, Jersey Joe Walcott, Rocky Marciano

92. INTERNATIONAL FLAVOR

1. (k)
2. (l)
3. (m)
4. (n)
5. (o)
6. (f)
7. (g)
8. (h)
9. (i)
10. (j)
11. (a)
12. (b)
13. (c)
14. (d)
15. (e)

93. INTERNATIONAL FLAVOR II

1. (f)
2. (g)
3. (h)
4. (i)
5. (j)
6. (a)
7. (b)
8. (c)
9. (d)
10. (e)

94. BOXING TIDBITS I

1. Middleweight Stan Ketchel, who was shot, and flyweight Pancho Villa, who died from a poisoned tooth
2. Archie Moore, 47. Fitzsimmons was next at 43 years
3. They both boxed barefoot due to a rain storm
4. They were all fifteen-round decisions
5. Pascual Perez, only 4 feet 11 inches

6. Angelo Dundee, who handled Ali, Pastrano (light-heavy) and Sugar Ramos (feather)
7. Denny Moyer
8. Battling Siki, who lost his title on a twenty-round decision to Mike McTigue on March 17, 1923
9. Charley Mitchell (158 pounds) vs. John L. Sullivan in 1888
10. Tommy Burns (172 pounds) and Jack O'Brien (163½ pounds) fought to a twenty-round draw in 1906
11. Primo Carnera (259½ pounds) recorded a fifteen-round win over Paolino Uzcudun (229¼ pounds) in 1933
12. Frazier in the first two, Ali in the third
13. Harry Wills. Dempsey's manager backed out of the fight
14. Muhammad Ali. Soccer player Pele was second in the balloting
15. In a motorcycle accident

95. BOXING TIDBITS II

1. Harry Greb and Tiger Flowers
2. Ted "Red Top" Davis
3. Johnny Buff
4. Georges Carpentier refereed Jack Johnson's title defenses against Andre Sproul and Frank Moran before meeting Jack Dempsey
5. Lightweight Al Singer won the title from Sammy Mandell and lost it to Tony Canzoneri in one-round bouts in 1930
6. Arthur Pelkey had this dramatic turn-around in his career after kayoing Luther McCarthy in one-round in Calgary, Canada in 1914
7. Jim Jeffries and Jersey Joe Walcott
8. Jackie Brown lost the British, European and world flyweight titles in two rounds to Benny Lynch in 1935
9. Benny Lynch beat Jackie Jurich in twelve rounds in a bout scheduled for the flyweight title in 1938
Lynch, however, was overweight, and some accepted Jurich as the champ
10. Greb won the title from Johnny Wilson (1923) and lost it to Tiger Flowers (1926), both in fifteen-round decisions

96. BOXING TIDBITS III

1. Nat Loubet
2. Jack Munroe
3. Jack Dempsey
4. Terry McGovern
5. Johnny Addie
6. Jim Driscoll
7. Nat Fleischer
8. Henry Armstrong
9. Nonpareil
10. Jack Root

126 / The World Championship Boxing Quizbook

97. PICK YOUR OWN TOP TEN

Give yourself 4 points for a correct first, 3 points for a correct second, and 1 point for getting any others in the top five right. (10 possible on each)

Listed in order:
1. *Heavyweights*: Dempsey, Louis, Johnson, Marciano, Jeffries, Ali, Tunney, Corbett, Frazier, Fitzsimmons
2. *LightHeavyweights*: Moore, Loughran, Foster, O'Brien, Conn, Dillon, Fitzsimmons, McCoy, Delaney, Berlenbach
3. *Middleweights*: Ketchel & Robinson (tied for first), Greb, Walker, Zale, Ryan, Cerdan, Papke, Fitzsimmons, Gibbons
4. *Welterweights*: Walcott, Armstrong, Robinson, Britton, Lewis, Ross, Napoles, Griffith, Smith, McLarnin
5. *Lightweights*: Leonard, Gans, Welsh, Canzoneri, Nelson, Ritchie, Armstrong, Lavigne & Ortiz (tied for eighth), Brown
6. *Featherweights*: McGovern, Pep, Atell, Driscoll, Chocolate, Saddler, Dundee, Kilbane, Armstrong, Griffo
7. *Bantamweights*: Herman, Jofre & Williams (tied for second), Dixon, Coulon, Lynch, Brown, Olivares, Escobar, Ortiz
8. *Flyweights*: Wilde, Villa, Genaro, LaBarba, Perez, Lynch, Buff & Wolgast & Kane (tied for seventh)
9. Armstrong's 2, 7 and 9 rankings beat Fitzsimmon's 7, 9 and 10 (10 points)
10. Sugar Ray Robinson, who tied for first as a middleweight and ranked third as a welterweight. It's hard to disagree

98. MUHAMMAD ALI SUPER QUIZ I

1. Crying on the shoulder of Louisville policeman and amateur boxing instructor Joe Martin, after discovering his bicycle was stolen
2. Twelve years old
3. Joe Martin (see number one), the policeman who ran Columbia Gym for six years
4. In his first bout on November 12, 1954. Ali was twelve years old, weighed 89 pounds, and stood four feet tall. He won a three-round split-decision over Ronie O'Keefe. The amateur boxing contest was carried over Louisville's WAVE-TV on Saturday night's "The Champions of Tomorrow."
5. Fred Stoner
6. Yes. Ali lost eight fights and won 100 as an amateur
7. Amos Johnson, who later turned pro
8. True. He was 376th out of the 391 students in his class
9. The light-heavyweight class
10. A border-line heavyweight, Ali felt that Italy's leading contender Fransesco De Piccoli would be favored by the Rome crowd. De Piccoli did win the heavy title
11. Australian Tony Madigan, who beat Ali only once in three meetings
12. True. He received quite a bit of attention for displaying his nationalistic pride
13. A syndicate of eleven Louisville businessmen led by Bill Faversham, Jr. included a pension in Ali's contract
14. One, an unimpressive six-round decision over Tunney Hunsaker
15. In 1957 when Dundee was in Louisville with his fighter Willie Pastrano. Ali met them and sparred one slick round with Pastrano. Ali was fifteen at the time

99. MUHAMMAD ALI SUPER QUIZ II

1. Ingemar Johansson, who was preparing to defend his title against Patterson
2. Prior to his sixth bout, Ali predicted a second-round knockout against Lamar Clark. He delivered the KO as promised
3. He appeared on a talk show with the wrestler Gorgeous George, and for once was not the star of the show. Ali then copied his show-offy style
4. Against Sonny Banks. Ali kayoed him in round four as he predicted, but was floored in the first round while prancing around
5. In his fight against Bailly Daniels
6. Alejandro Lavorante, who Ali stopped in five rounds in 1962
7. Archie Moore, who fell in four
8. Shortly before the Doug Jones bout
9. The close decision (5-4, 5-4, 8-1) over Doug Jones in Madison Square Garden
10. Henry Cooper, in round four, before being stopped in round five
11. He had liniment in his eyes and wanted to quit, but manager Dundee forced him out into the ring
12. The next day
13. Malcolm X
14. Jany didn't see the first-round KO punch. Referee Jersey Joe Walcott made matters worse by losing track of the completed knockout count
15. Ali insulted the well-liked Patterson, then toyed around with him in the ring

100. MUHAMMAD ALI SUPER QUIZ III

1. The Canadian referee allowed Chuvalo at least 100 low blows without a warning during the fifteen-round bout
2. German Karl Mildenberger, who lasted twelve rounds
3. The W.B.A., because he fought a return match with Sonny Liston
4. He won nearly every round in winning a fifteen-round decision
5. A seven-round KO over Zora Folley on March 22, 1967
6. *Ring* magazine
7. Over four years. He refused induction on April 28, 1967 and was exonerated June 28, 1971
8. Jerry Quarry. He stopped Jerry in the third round of their October 26, 1970 fight
9. A fifteen-round TKO victory over Oscar Bonavena
10. It marked the first time two undefeated champs ever met in the ring
11. Eight rounds
12. In his five bouts before meeting Foreman (1973-74), Ali settled for five straight twelve-round decisions over Joe Bugner, Ken Norton (twice), Rudy Lubbers, and Joe Frazier
13. In San Diego, Norton's home-town. The split-decision loss would probably have been no worse than a draw anywhere else
14. Their first two meetings took place in Madison Square Garden, the third in Manila, Philippines
15. Frazier, in the fifteenth round of their first bout
16. Chuck Wepner, in round nine of his fifteenth-round TKO loss to Ali. The champ claimed it was a slip
17. Ron Lyle
18. Liston, Quarry, Chuvalo, Patterson, Bugner, Norton, and Cooper

19. Yes. A hernia operation forced postponement of his title defense against Sonny Liston
20. There is no end to the material about a man who became a legend in his own time. Even as an 89-pound weakling he was on TV. He will be recorded in history as the greatest heavyweight champion who ever lived.

THE VERDICT

Time to tally up all your points so the judges and referee can reach their decision.

- 0—250   You've been knocked out cold in the first round—Time to hang up the gloves.
- 251—500   You barely laid a glove on him in losing a unanimous decision—Have you ever considered a safer career?
- 501—750   You came out on the short end of a split-decision—Back to the gym.
- 751—1000   You pulled out a close decision in the late rounds with a furious flurry—There's hope yet for a title shot.
- 1001—1210   Referee stops the fight . . . 2:10 seconds of the fifth round . . . Winner by a technical knockout and new World Boxing Quiz Champion—YOU!!